CREEPOLOGY

SELF-DEFENSE FOR YOUR SOCIAL LIFE

D1737184

A.R. BANKS

For updates, new releases, useful links, and other information, please check out:

https://godsbastard.wordpress.com/

CONTENTS

FOREWORD BY RORY MILLER

Most self-defense training isn't appropriate for the real world. I'm not talking techniques that would never work, taught by people who have never used them. The problem is more fundamental.

This might be over generalizing (a bit) but standard self-defense is taught as a collection of unrealistically complex solutions to unrealistically simple problems. So instructors focus on "stranger danger" when domestic violence is much more prevalent. They teach techniques against multiple opponents and never even consider what might happen if you injure a gang member while your whole family has to live in that gang's territory. All situations have consequences and context.

Self-defense, as a rule, is not just aimed at the problems of middle-class privileged people. It's aimed at the imaginary problems of middle-class privileged people.

One subject instructors rarely address – creepers. They are the low level sexual predators that make so many women's lives miserable, yet are invisible to most men. This is a real problem, not an imaginary one. It's not the active shooter or the stranger jumping out of the bushes, which most people will never experience. Creepers are a problem that someone you know is dealing with right now.

Most instructors hand-wave past the complex stuff. It's easy to teach what to do – legally and physically – when a stranger raises his hand against you. Much harder to teach what you can do – legally, physically and socially – about the guy who just happens to rub up against you whenever no one is watching.

A.R. Banks has taken on this complex subject in this little book. For the people dealing with creeps, it's invaluable advice. For people teaching self-defense, it's a wake-up call.

Read this one.

ACKNOWLEDGEMENTS

With many thanks to Rory Miller, who encouraged me to write this even when it really, really sucked.

To Mary Kogut, who cheered all the way along and spotted countless typos.

To Shane Michael Murphy, who still hasn't learnt when to duck.

To Kelley Hanson Haeder, Kaja Sadowski, and Edward Hines, who suffered through the first draft or chunks thereof.

To Kasey Keckeisen, who gave me the opportunity to run this program at the Violence Dynamics seminar.

And to countless creeps who gave me and still give me tons of practical experience.

INTRODUCTION

"No one has a social obligation to be victimized."
– Joe Navarro

THE CREEPY GUY NARRATIVE

This is such a common story that it's become a cliché.

A woman meets a man. He may be a casual acquaintance; someone she met on public transport or at a shop. He may be a member of her social network; someone from work, school, a club or social activity, or a neighbor. The guy doesn't sit quite right with her. Sometimes there's something about him that bothers her right from the start. Sometimes things start out OK, but soon she becomes uncomfortable.

She can't really say what it is about him that unsettles her so much. Perhaps there is something unnerving about the way he looks at her, staring at her too intently, or constantly looking at her out of the corner of his eyes. He may stand too close, or accidentally (yet conveniently) keep being in her way so that they have to brush against each other. He may seem too familiar in his physical contact; shaking hands for too long, insisting on hugs when everyone else just shakes hand, or insisting on kisses when everyone else just hugs. He may give her compliments that seem too personal. He may open up to her too much, revealing personal details that she would have preferred to be ignorant of.

He may seek her presence more than their connection warrants, or linger near her after whatever business they may have is concluded. He may track her down in settings outside of their connection. If he is a colleague, he might suddenly turn up at her gym or her house, or track her down online. If he is a neighbor, he might turn up at her work. Although he always has a valid reason for his presence – nobody could accuse him of stalking – the fact that he keeps turning up is starting to concern her. Conversely, he may only ever be where he's supposed to be, but the likelihood of his presence makes her dread that place.

Whatever he is doing, his behavior is just ever-so-slightly off. Nothing that seems serious. Nothing she can put a finger on. Nothing that makes sense when she tries to articulate it, even to herself. Definitely nothing she could get any outside help with. What is she going to tell people, that a guy smiles at her too much and she wants them to get him to stop?

All and still, there is something not quite right about him, and she feels that keenly. What freaks her out even more is that he seems to be ignoring her discomfort. She knows that she is sending all the subtle negative signals she can think of, but he doesn't seem to be reading them. She's definitely not encouraging him, yet he seems to be getting keener.

She might talk to her partner, friends, or colleagues about him. She might be told that he's a bit odd, but harmless. That he doesn't really mean it. That that's just the way he is. She might be told off for being so judgmental. The poor guy is just an awkward fellow who is doing his best; he just keeps messing up. She might be told that she needs to cut him some slack. She might be called "stuck-up" or a "bitch" for insisting that she hates to have him near her. She might be told that it's partly her fault: she must have led him on, and now he believes they're friends, or more than friends. What is she going to do now? Turn on him and hurt his feelings? Is she really that kind of person?

She might be told that everything is OK. That her feelings on the subject are plain wrong, that she is seeing things that are not there, or that she is making a mountain out of a molehill. She can't really say that those naysayers are wrong; after all, the guy hasn't done anything that bad. She can't point to any one thing that justifies how she feels: nervous, fearful, besieged, sullied. Creeped out. Those feelings make no sense, but they will not go away.

Whenever she thinks about him, her brain starts spinning. Half of her is busy trying to work out what is really going on. Is the guy really OK? Is he dangerous, and just biding his time? The other half of her is obsessing about the possible repercussions of misinterpreting the situation. If she over-reacts and the guy is an innocent dork, her entire social group will punish her for it. If she under-reacts and the guy is a predator, there is no knowing what he could do to her.

On the outside she carries on as normal. On the inside, however, her brain is constantly ruminating on the issue, never coming to a definite conclusion. The guy may be taking up a tiny part of her day, yet he is consuming a huge amount of her mental energy. She knows she is allowing him to live rent-free in her head, but she can't stop it. She is stuck waiting for an answer: for proof that she is safe or for the other shoe to drop.

PUPPET IN A PLAY

Every creep is an individual. However, the Creepy Guy Narrative is precisely that: a narrative, and not even a particularly creative one. Although each retelling of the story will feel special at the time and will present some variations, certain common elements are almost always present. By learning to identify those common elements, we can teach ourselves to recognize when the narrative is being woven around us. We can also learn how to unravel the tale, or turn it into our own story, leading to the ending we choose.

The first thing we need to accept is that the Creepy Guy Narrative is not an unfortunate series of accidental trespasses upon our person. It is a strategy: a plan of action designed to achieve a specific aim. The creep is consciously doing this to us. He might be doing it deliberately, to make us feel awful, or negligently, as the by-product of a deeply selfish seduction strategy. Either way, he is aware that he is making us uncomfortable and that is not enough to make him stop.

The creep's strategy consists of carefully organized and practiced moves arranged to achieve the maximum effect for minimum risk. The reason so many creeps seem to engage in similar patterns of behavior is that those patterns reliably work.

The strategy is predicated on sowing and exploiting doubt, both in our head and in our support group. The uncertainty we feel is not caused by any inadequacy on our part: it is part and parcel of the strategy.

The reason most creeps never seem to get anywhere with their game is that they already are where they want to be. Low-level predators may never escalate. If all they want is our time and attention, they've got it. If they get off on our confusion, fear, and revulsion, they've got it. Our discomfort is either insignificant to them, or it's precisely what they want.

For those of us who enjoy getting on with people, or who want people to like us, this may be very hard to accept. It's even harder to accept that some people get so much enjoyment out of hurting others emotionally that they will shape their entire public persona in order to be able to do so without the risk of retribution.

Although a creep does not assault us physically, he is still a predator. He is simply a predator who chooses to use non-physical means to hunt us. Assaulting people physically can carry heavy social and legal costs. Badgering them for attention or hurting them emotionally, on the other hand, is relatively risk-free. It may not be as satisfying, but he can do it again tomorrow, and the day after, and the day after that.

Once a creep has selected us as his target, we are likely to remain so unless steps are taken to change the situation. While he is getting what he wants out of us, and while he is safe and comfortable in doing so, he has no reason to quit.

The strategy relies on social mechanisms pre-installed in women's brains throughout our upbringing to keep us stuck in a fear-induced freeze. In many cultures, women are raised to be "nice" first and foremost, to prioritize other people's feelings, not to speak out, not to make a fuss. Women who break those rules are "bitches" and may suffer socially as a result. Being concerned about these social costs can stop women from protecting themselves.

Although the situation may feel personal, it isn't. The story woven around us is not about us as individuals. We have merely been selected as participants because, in the creep's eyes, we meet whichever criteria he deems necessary for the story to work. This isn't about us. It's merely happening at us.

The reason the Creepy Guy Narrative is so common is that it is incredibly successful. There are so many creeps around because being a creep is a low-risk, high benefit game.

The only way we can change this is to change the odds of the game: increase the stakes and lower the chances of success. We may not be able to do this society-wide unless we're Batman, but we can push in that direction, and we can make it happen for ourselves and our immediate social group.

The strengths of the creep's strategy are also its downfall. The strategy is entirely predicated on us following the script laid down before us. We are expected to respond in predictable ways to a series of inputs. By responding *in any other way*, we can make the whole strategy fall apart.

The strategy requires us to be confused and unsure. By seeing and accepting the situation for what it is, we take away that confusion. We can then spend our time and energy in dealing with the situation, instead of treading water. This, on its own, can improve our position in a way the creep had not anticipated.

The strategy uses social pressure and the fear of social or professional punishment to keep us suffering in silence. It requires us to feel isolated and unsupported, sometimes even socially obliged to put up with the creep's behavior. By learning to cultivate a healthy support group and to involve the people around us in the situation, we can completely change our social landscape. Instead of being able to isolate us from our social resources, the creep may find our entire social group turning against him. In situations where that is not possible, we can free ourselves of this yoke by learning not to care about those who, ultimately, do not care about us.

The strategy requires that we respond with discomfort or fear to the creep's activities. By manifesting *any other emotional response*, we can stop the creep from getting what he wants. In fact, by selecting certain emotional responses, we can turn the tables on our creep. We can, if we so choose, predate on our predator.

ON GENDER

This book is written entirely with a gender bias: men as predators or parasites, women as targets. I am deliberately ignoring every other permutation of the problem. That's not because those permutations don't occur or are not significant; it's because I can only write about what I know, and my experience is affected by the gender people assume me to be and the expectations that stem from that assumption.

Gender is still a huge deal in our society. Gender prejudices and expectations are all around us. Our gender affects how people relate to us, our victim profile, the resources and strategies we can use, and how our actions will be judged by our social group. While other gender systems exist, our society mainly functions along binary lines. Most people will knock us into one category or another, even if that's not where we put ourselves.

Gender also shapes what we see and experience. I have a ton of experience in male-on-female predation and parasitism. I know very little of every other permutation; I haven't experienced it, I haven't seen it unfold, and I've not dealt with it.

I know that female creeps who prey on men exist because men relate this kind of experience, but those women don't swim in my waters. I don't see them doing their thing, so I don't know what "their thing" looks like. I don't know how to best deal with them. I don't know whether the self-protection strategies women can use would work well for men – or, if they do, at what cost – because gender expectations affect the effectiveness of those strategies.

Men often get the worst end of the deal when it comes to the aftermath, too. Men tend to have little or no social and structural support against a predatory woman. Their experiences and needs do not fit the common narrative, so they get ignored. No woman will go to her girlfriends to report a sexual assault and be told "Oh, that's so cool, was he hot?" Men do. It happens all the time. And it's even worse when it comes to seeking official support. Not only would a man be less likely to be believed or taken seriously than a woman, but it would be possible for the tables to be turned on him. It is feasible for a woman to perv on a guy and, if he threatened repercussions or simply out of spite, report him for perving on her. The opposite is highly unlikely. That's a huge degree of power right there, and some women are willing to yield it for evil.

One of the reasons the common narrative is so deeply gendered is that people like me continue to present only one side of the issue. As a result, there is an increasing amount of pressure in some quarters to remove all references to gender when discussing this kind of issue. I understand what this pressure is trying to achieve; it's high time we stopped assuming that in a situation between a woman and a man, the man must be the aggressor. However, to treat these kinds of issues as if gender was not an issue – as if men and women faced the same problems with the same resources – is to willfully ignore reality. Such measures may reduce the problem in the long term, but they do very little to equip people with effective tools to deal with the problem here and now. Any gender-neutral solution we may come up with is likely to fail against the onslaught of the gender bias under which we live.

I can only talk about one specific, binary-biased experience, but that doesn't make the experience useless to people who do not fit into that category. I hope this book will be of some help to people of all genders, dealing with creeps of all genders. Each of them will have to find what works for them and what doesn't, but that is true of all of us, regardless of gender: there is no cookie-cutter solution to the creep problem.

I hope that one day soon effective support will be available to everyone, regardless of gender. All permutations of the creep narrative should be addressed, and none should be tolerated.

GOALS

This book has very specific goals. It aims to teach women:

- To distinguish between low-level sexual predators and other personalities (in particular "just socially awkward" people) who may manifest in the same way.
- To understand that low-level predation is scripted.
- To manipulate that script to our advantage.
- To learn a variety of strategies for neutralizing low-level predators.
- To engineer a personal plan for dealing with the low-level predators and sundry assholes in our lives, selecting the tactics that best suit us.

This book does not aim to cover a broad spectrum of self-defense needs and tactics. It focuses solely on low-level sexual predators operating in physically safe situations. The tactics and techniques we will be looking at are strictly non-physical.

This book does not aim to teach you to respond to physically unsafe situations. If you are at risk of imminent physical or sexual assault or in a physically unsafe situation (for instance if you are alone with a potential predator and there is no way to quickly summon help), that is not the time to try and work out the underlying psychology and strategy of your threat. **Make yourself safe first.**

WHAT ARE WE TALKING ABOUT?

Most women will have to deal with a creepy guy at some point in their lives. Some of us go through the experience multiple times. Many of us find ourselves having to deal with him alone, unable to get any help either from our support network or from the authorities. We often find it hard to articulate the problem, even to ourselves. Talking about it to third parties seems hopeless, and when we try we often fail to convey what is really going on and why it is so important to us.

That's not a failure on our part: it's a result of the strategy used by the creeps. Creeps are hard to talk about because what they do is hard to pin down; that's why they can keep doing it. If they escalated to overt, punishable behaviors, chances are that they would get punished. Creeps thrive in ambiguity and confusion.

The situation isn't helped by the fact that terms like "creep" are incredibly ambiguous. The word is used to describe so many personalities, behaviors, and situations that it ends up meaning completely different things to different people, ultimately meaning nothing.

For instance, we can compare these definitions:

From the Oxford Dictionaries:[1]

> **creep**
> Pronunciation: /kriːp/
> NOUN
> *informal* A detestable person:
> *I thought he was a nasty little creep*
> A person who behaves obsequiously in the hope of advancement.
> **give someone the creeps**
> *informal* Induce a feeling of revulsion or fear in someone:
> *eels wriggle, they're slimy, and they give some people the creeps*
> **creep someone out**
> *informal* Give someone an unpleasant feeling of fear or unease:
> *an anonymous note like that would creep me out*

---

[1] http://www.oxforddictionaries.com/definition/english/creep

From Urban Dictionary: [2]

> **creep**
> A dude who tries way too hard with chicks, usually younger chicks. Also usually waits till the chicks are fucked up to take advantage of them.
>
> A man or woman who breaks social rules in an odd or frightening way. Ironically, those who use this word the most are often somewhat creepy themselves.
>
> A weird guy who nobody likes/loves/wants.
>
> An awesome song by Radiohead... meaning something like loser, or not good enough for someone you love... being weird, and strange.
>
> A creep is a male that a female is not interested in. A woman may label a man a creep if the man does not communicate to her that he has wealth, power, or influence (such as by the clothes he wears, the car he drives, the job title he carries, or other external signs of social proof), and the only thing he does show to her, his physical attractiveness, is not enough to interest her.

All these definitions of "creep," although hardly similar and somewhat different in the level of authority they carry, are correct: the word is indeed used in all those contexts. Men are called creeps for engaging in a variety of unpleasant behaviors, both accidentally and on purpose. Men are also unfairly called creeps for engaging in behaviors that, if carried out by more attractive men, would be considered perfectly acceptable.

If the word "creep" is used without any additional information, it's entirely possible that the person hearing it will completely misunderstand the issue in question. This is particularly true if we are talking to somebody who has no direct experience of the creep problem.

---

[22] http://www.urbandictionary.com/define.php?term=creep

WHAT IS A CREEP?

This book aims to help women deal with creeps first by clarifying the nature of the problem, and then by providing a series of possible solutions. We will be dealing with a very specific type of person, who engages in a very specific type of behavior for a specific goal:

> **In this context, a <u>creep</u> is a person who <u>consciously</u> behaves in a manner likely to give someone an unpleasant feeling of fear or unease, specifically where there is a sexual undercurrent to that discomfort.**

The key word here is "consciously." There are tons of reasons why a person may make us feel uncomfortable. They could be socialized differently from us, poorly socialized, or unable to read or respond to non-verbal cues. Sometimes things between people just go awry through miscommunication. For instance, someone could be staring at our lips while we are talking and that could make us very uncomfortable, but all they are doing is trying to lip-read because they are hard of hearing. That kind of accidental, unintentional discomfort isn't what this book is about: for the purpose of this exercise, a creep is someone who *consciously* does things that makes us uncomfortable.

A creep's behavior and the creeped-out feelings that behavior causes are his only distinguishing features. Creeps are not uniform in appearance. They don't all look, dress, live, or carry themselves a certain way. Some may make efforts to stick out from the norm while others may blend in to the point of being virtually invisible. We cannot rely on looks, style, socio-economic status, age, or anything of the kind to determine whether someone is a creep or not. Platitudes notwithstanding, a "neck beard" or a fedora do not suffice as identification features.

The only thing all creeps have in common is what they do: they consciously creep people out. The million dollar question is: why would they do that? Particularly if they have designs of a sexual nature on us, why would they want to make us uncomfortable? Generally speaking, making someone want to vomit or run off is not a prelude to a fulfilling relationship, or even to sexytime. So why do the creeps do it?

MOTIVATIONS FOR CREEPING

Creeps creep consciously, not accidentally. There are two main motivations behind their behavior:

Negligent Creeps **make women uncomfortable by putting their own sexual desires ahead of women's interests and comfort.** These guys don't set out to deliberately creep anyone out, but they behave in ways that they know will cause women to be creeped out on the off-chance that it might get them laid. **The creeped-out feeling is a by-product of their seduction strategy.**

I originally started writing about creeps in reaction to an article on a popular dating advice column teaching men how to approach women wearing headphones in a public place. I am not going to link to the original article because I don't want to draw traffic to it. The specific article is irrelevant, anyway, because the number of sites pushing this kind of advice is staggering. I found this particular article irksome because it specifically encouraged men to ignore their target's signals and behavior and prioritize their sexual needs. Personally, if I'm on the rowing machine at the gym with my headphones on, the last thing I need is some bright spark stopping me because he feels moved to tell me how attracted he is to me.[3] Not every woman feels the same, but it is a very common sentiment. It's not an inappropriate sentiment, either, because that kind of behavior says a lot about the psychology of the guy in question. I might not know anything else about him, but I know that he puts his own interests ahead of mine. That, to me, is not an attractive characteristic.

Back when that article went out, a multitude of women writers wrote their responses, most of which riffed on the theme of "don't": if you see a woman out in public clearly busy doing her thing, in a place that isn't normally construed as a mating area, and giving clear signs that she wants to be left alone, *let her be*. Aside from the very good chance that your advances will make her feel uncomfortable, you are probably the umpteenth guy to bother her. Your chances of success are pretty low, while your chances of making the object of your desires feel uncomfortable or even threatened are pretty high.

The responses from some of the guys were interesting. There seemed to be two main camps. Some guys insisted that if women go out and about looking attractive – not necessarily in revealing clothing, but just looking

---

[3] Yes, that actually happened.

pretty – then they must be doing so to get attention from guys. It couldn't be that women just enjoy looking nice, that being nicely turned out is a requirement of their job, or that the gods cursed them with being pretty. These guys believe that women are being pretty *at* them. If these women cruelly spurn the attention they get as a result of their choice, then they're cockteases. If that attention makes them uncomfortable, too bad: they're only getting what they deserve. So, although these guys don't go out with the intention of bothering women, they don't care that they are doing so and there is a component of malevolence to their attitude.

Other guys were allegedly horrified at the suggestion that their advances may be perceived as threatening, or even bothersome. That was never their intention. Their logic is that they would really like it if women threw themselves at them, so why wouldn't women feel the same? I have lost count of how many conversations I've been involved in between dudes who kept insisting that women should just learn to like this, and women explaining the reasons why they don't. The vast majority of the times, the result was that the dudes accepted that what they were doing had a low chance of success and a high chance of making women uncomfortable. However, they were going to carry on regardless, because you never know your luck. If doing something gives them a one-in-a-million chance of getting laid, it's worth a shot. The cost, in the form of the 999,999 women they are bothering in the process, just doesn't register with them. It doesn't bother them to bother women. And anyway, that's how their hero gets the girl in their favorite movie, and Hollywood never lies!

This attitude may seem benign. These guys do not go out with the intention of upsetting women, let alone harming them. Their selfishness is problematic, though, particularly in the context of ongoing social relationships, when our connection is not just a one-off event.

These guys believe that their needs and wants trump other people's needs and wants. In a sexual context, this is the attitude of a potential consent violator.

They are not guys we want to go out for a drink with, or be in a room alone with. They are not guys we want escorting us back to our car because the car park is dark. People's behavior generally worsens as the stakes increase. The closer these guys get to a chance of getting laid, the pushier and less considerate they are likely to become. I'm not saying they're all potential rapists, but they are the kind of guys who don't mind pushing a little bit against our consent or trying to circumvent it.

These are the "nicer" creeps. These are the guys who set out to seduce us, not creep us out. They creep us out of carelessness or selfishness, but not on purpose. Their creeping is aggressive panhandling for sex, not a game in itself. There are worse guys out there.

Malignant Creeps are low-level sexual predators who creep women out deliberately. These creeps engage in certain behaviors precisely because they know that it will make women feel repulsed or threatened. They are bona fide predators, even if they never go physical. They are doing as much as they can to get their kicks without doing anything overt or illegal. **The creeped-out feeling is the goal of their activities.**

Being a predator carries a lot of risk. These guys are clever enough to scale their activities down to whatever will not get them into trouble while still giving them what they want; and what they want is women's fear. That's what they feed on.

The question again is why: why would they want to make someone feel threatened? Quite simply, some people get off on that. There are people who commit sexual assaults not because of the sex per se, but because they enjoy dominating people, causing them pain and fear. The sex may be an important part of the act, but the value of the act is in the power they can exert, or the amount of pain and fear they can cause. Think about it: if it was only the sex they were after, they could just hire a professional. The cost of paid encounters varies between locations, but I can guarantee you that it's a hell of a lot cheaper than risking prison time on the off-chance of getting to rub bits with a stranger against their will.

For some people creeping is a way to get a small dose of that power, to be able to inflict a bit of that pain, in a safe way – a way that makes them able to do it all again tomorrow. It's not the same buzz as attacking someone, but provided that they don't push it too far, they could do it for the rest of their living days without having to fear any kind of repercussion.

All creeps cross the line between what is socially acceptable and what isn't; that's why they make us uncomfortable. Negligent Creeps do so consciously but not intentionally, out of selfishness rather than malevolence. Malignant Creeps do so both consciously *and* deliberately. If they've got us terrified and confused, they've got us where they want us and they'll do their best to keep us there as long as they can.

SOCIAL GRAY AREAS

The main reason why creeps are so hard to spot and eradicate is that, if they are any good, their game is subtle. They play in the gray areas between what is socially acceptable and what is legally actionable.

Some interpersonal behaviors in our society are regulated by law. For instance, if I grab someone by the crotch without their consent I've committed a sexual assault. If I email a work colleague with whom I've not previously mutually flirted a list of the sexual acts I'd like to carry out with them, I've committed sexual harassment. Whether I would be punished and how seriously depends on a variety of factors. I might get away with it. However, I run the risk that someone in a position of authority is going to want to talk to me about it. I could be charged with a crime. I could lose my job. Unless my social network is accepting of this kind of behavior, I could lose my social status and my support group. There are serious potential consequences to misbehaving in actionable ways.

The bulk of interpersonal behavior, though, is not regulated by law, but by unspoken social conventions. For instance, we don't have laws stipulating how to say hello to people. Depending on where we live, we might shake hands or hug. If we hug, we might give an A-frame hug, with only the top of the bodies making contact, or we might squash ourselves right against a person. If we greet someone wrong, unless we commit an assault in the process there won't be any official repercussions. However, if the way in which we greet someone is not appropriate to the situation, the person at the receiving end of it will feel uncomfortable. They may or may not feel threatened, depending on how threatening we are. They will almost certainly be left wondering what the hell is going on, though, and the event may weigh on their minds long after it is over.

The beauty of this tactic is that it can be customized to fit the occasion. There are endless ways to be ever-so-slightly inappropriate. Furthermore, it can be done so subtly that not even the person directly at the receiving end of it will be able to tell what exactly is wrong, if anything really is. That level of subtlety can add an element of gaslighting to the occasion: if the target asks bystanders if they've noticed anything wrong, chances are that they haven't. The target could end up questioning not only the situation, but her own memory, perception, and sanity. Adding drugs or alcohol to the mixture can blur the situation even further.

Conversely, in creep-friendly or creep-oblivious environments, a creep can turn the game up a few notches, delighting in behaving obviously inappropriately and getting away with it.

WHY IS CREEPING SO LOW-RISK?

There is a consistent element to all types and styles of creeping: they work. Creeping is a low reward, but low risk endeavor. Successful creeps are perfectly able to infiltrate an environment and stay there indefinitely without repercussions. Their presence may result in a whole bunch of women leaving that space, yet the creeps persist, happy as the proverbial pigs in the muck.

The main reason creeping is so successful is that it can be extremely hard to conclusively identify a creep. We have spoken so far of two main types of creeps, separated by their motivations. That kind of classification is all very good in theory, but in real life it doesn't work well because most people are not mind-readers. It can be hard or even impossible to determine *why* someone is behaving as they are, particularly in the moment. So if the reasons why matter to us, we can end up waiting forever for enough information and never take any action.

Identifying a creep conclusively becomes even more difficult when we consider how easy it can be to creep people out accidentally. A real creep acts consciously, but there is a variety of reasons why people may creep us out not only unintentionally but sometimes without even knowing that they are doing so:

- They may be socialized differently from us. For instance, they might belong to a different culture or subculture.
- They may have been improperly socialized due to shortcomings in their parenting or schooling.
- They may have a condition that makes it difficult or impossible for them to operate within social norms.
- They may be unable to read or respond to non-verbal cues.
- They may be unable to detect or express emotions.
- They could remind us of someone who creeped us out in the past.
- We might dislike their mannerisms or appearance, even though there is nothing intrinsically "wrong" with them.
- They could simply be more extroverted or introverted than us, so we read them as over-friendly or antisocial.

These people may not be doing anything *at* us: the issue may be with the way they interact with the world. Moreover, unless we communicate our displeasure to them, they might have no idea that their actions are causing us any discomfort, because they are not mind readers, either.

I personally don't class those people as creeps, even though I feel creeped out by them. The fact that they are doing it unconsciously matters to me; that's where *I* draw the line between someone who is a creep and someone who isn't. It is my line and my choice. That doesn't mean that that's where *you* should draw that line: it's up to *you* to decide that. But that line – the difference between someone who is just doing something and someone who is doing it *at* us – is what stops a lot of people from taking any kind of action when they feel creeped out. We are so worried about accidentally upsetting those who don't mean to do anything wrong that we end up taking no steps against those who do.

The result is an effortless victory on the creeps' part. Even people who detest the mere thought of creeps can end up coexisting with them, sometimes for extended periods of time. It's not the awkwardness or risk of having to deal with the creeps that stops them taking action; it's the fear of that action being unwarranted, of making a fuss over nothing, of being mean to someone who "didn't mean it like that," of ending up the bad person in the story. We can be so invested in protecting the innocent that we totally fail to deal with the guilty. This allows people who creep consciously, genuine creeps, to continue their activities without repercussions.

Creeps derive a large chunk of their power from other people protecting them. This is often hailed as an example of rape culture – of prevailing social attitudes that normalize or trivialize sexual assault and harassment. Some groups do allow wide degrees of creeping, particularly creeping on "lesser" humans, because to them it's acceptable. The bulk of that protection, however, is often due to nice people's unwillingness to be mean.

Until there is conclusive evidence that an individual is creeping on purpose, most people don't want to think ill of him, let alone take steps against him. Once an individual has developed a reputation for being consistently a little bit odd, a little bit awkward, most people will go out of their way to make sure that his behavior is evaluated by its own special set of metrics. Everything he does is OK, even when it's socially inappropriate and makes people deeply uncomfortable, because it's him doing it. "You know what he's like!"

It gets worse. Once an individual has established himself as the local socially awkward person, anyone who picks on him is a bad person. It doesn't matter whether their complaints are valid: they are picking on a poor puppy who can't help himself, so they're obviously at fault. The creep has groomed the group into not only tolerating, but protecting him.

CREEP HAVENS

Creeps can be found in most environments: parks, trains, workplaces, shops, churches, gyms, and virtually any kind of club or society. Any place where people may turn up can attract its share of creeps. However, there are some environments that are particularly attractive to this kind of critter:

- Where they can reliably find their targets of choice.
- Where they can creep without being spotted or punished.

Target availability is essential to the creep. If they prey on women, for instance, frequenting environments where no women are present will not meet their requirements. They need to find or create the opportunity to access their targets. Such opportunity can be created by physical proximity (e.g. joining a workplace or club, going to a shop, etc.), or by just having a way to contact the targets (e.g. joining an internet forum, obtaining a phone number, etc.).

In environments where no targets are available the creeps' behavior may be entirely unremarkable. This can create a degree of uncertainty in their identification: people who have seen them in a target-free environment may find it hard to accept that their behavior can be completely different around their targets.

However, mere access to targets is not enough. In order to avoid detection, the access needs to be justified: the creeps need a valid reason to be there. They need to become the kind of person whose presence around those targets seems warranted, or at least acceptable.

For instance, a man wishing to look at unconsenting naked women could simply stroll into the ladies' changing rooms at the local pool. However, that is unlikely to end well. People are likely to notice and react, sometimes dramatically. It is not a behavior that can be easily explained away and the repercussions can be severe.

Justified access reduces the risk of repercussion; if a creep has a right to be in a place, his behavior may still be called into question, but his presence won't. Justified access can be obtained in a number of ways. The amount of effort needed to obtain it will depend on how specific a game the creep in question is playing.

A creep that contents himself with rubbing against strangers, for instance, needs do nothing more than using public transport at peak times. By contrast, a creep who wants to create a personal "relationship" with his targets, or to target a group that is usually protected (e.g. children) will need to work harder. For an extreme example, pedophile Scout leaders and the like aren't unfortunate souls who, wishing to help children, find themselves inexplicably and uncontrollably sexually attracted to them. They are people who specifically worked at getting justified access to their targets of choice.

The better a creep's cover is – the more justification he has for the access he is misusing – the harder it will be for his targets not only to avoid him, but also to call him out or punish him.

Spaces or groups where creeps can gain justified access to their targets of choice and continue their creeping unchecked can become **creep havens**. There are four group traits that make this more likely:

1. **Groups where normally inappropriate touching is allowed.**
   If we go to a tango class we can expect strangers to stand close to us and touch us in ways that would be inappropriate outside that setting. In that kind of situation it can be hard to draw the line between what's normally inappropriate but normal here, and what's just all-round inappropriate.

   Under these circumstances it can be difficult for a target to get any support. The inappropriateness of the touch can be so minute that it can be tough to convince anyone that there really is an issue, and almost impossible to get that issue addressed. The burden of proof is firmly on the target, who has to demonstrate that the creep crossed a sometimes very fine line. This can be incredibly hard to do. The question in many people's minds will be "if they don't like being touched, why do they come here at all?"

2. **Groups that value tolerance (in the form of inclusiveness, acceptance, or permissiveness) above all.**
   If one of the core values of the group is that people should be accepted precisely as they are, this can bleed into the group believing that people have a right to behave any way they like. All behaviors must be tolerated, no matter their impact on third parties. Anyone who suggests that some behaviors are inappropriate or even who simply asks not to be exposed to those behaviors is seen as intolerant and may be punished. Ironically, these groups are intolerant of what they class as intolerance, and happy to ostracize ostracizers.

   This attitude is often held by groups composed of people who suffered ostracism from other groups, such as nerd communities. It can be very hard for such a group to accept that their core values have contributed to creating a situation that is now causing one or more of their members to suffer. It can be even harder for those groups to accept that actions that go against those core values may be required.

3. Groups that pride themselves on being separate from the mainstream.

Some groups are proud to make their own rules, sometimes deliberately going against mainstream social conventions. It doesn't matter whether they are outlaw biker gangs or Klingon dating clubs; the key factor here is that being outside the norm is a key part of the group's identity.

The more special these groups believe they are, the less inclined they'll be to bow down to social conventions. People who try to bring external rules into play are treated as outsiders to the group or oppressors.

4. Groups that pride themselves on being the sort of places where that kind of thing just doesn't happen.

The classic example of this is a church. Religious people aren't perverts, right? So this kind of thing can't possibly happen here. Whistleblowers threaten the image of the entire church, so they are not only disbelieved, but often punished. Precisely the same dynamic can apply in kink groups if participants become so focused on protecting themselves from unjust allegations that they end up burying just allegations too.

The issue is further complicated if more than one core value is involved. Their effects accumulate, making the space even better for creeps. For instance, a group priding itself on being an accepting place for people struggling with social skills and being sexually permissive may find it very difficult to establish and enforce rules that punish people for being awkward around sex.

The important thing to remember in these situations is that the fault is not with the group's characteristics and values, but with the creeps who are deliberately exploiting them for their own convenience. The problem isn't that tango requires people to touch each other, that swimming pools allow mix-gender sessions, or that clubs welcome new members. The problem is that creeps are willing and able to exploit those factors in order to plague their targets.

One of the things people tend to forget – or deliberately sweep under the carpet – is that mixed-gender self-defense and martial arts classes can provide all of these elements. Most clubs are inclusive; people can literally walk in off the street. Mainstream social norms do not apply. Touching people in all manners of inappropriate ways is in-built into the activity;

this is particularly true of classes that involve grappling, but it's not exclusive to them. And no creep would ever dare show his face here, right?

Joining a self-defense class can provide creeps with the justified access to their targets of choice. The fact that it is hard to believe that anyone would be so daring makes it easier for creeps to go unnoticed and work unchecked.

WHAT'S THE BIG DEAL?

The transgressions creeps make tend to fit in one of three categories:
- Minor deviations from "normal" behaviors (e.g. hugging too tightly).
- Major deviations from "normal" behaviors which are classed as social gaffes (e.g. volunteering the details of one's sexual preferences over a work lunch).
- Actionable behaviors delivered in a setting where it's hard to prove that they took place (e.g. making threatening sexual comments in a crowded room where nobody else can hear them).

Creeps do whatever they can get away with. They might stand too close, but never touch. They may touch, but always make it look like an accident. They may seek out situations where touching is appropriate, but carry it just a little bit too far. They may say something in an inappropriate tone, but using perfectly appropriate words. They may say something utterly inappropriate, but in a setting where nobody will believe they did it. None of these transgressions are punishable by law. In our culture, many aren't even punishable by custom. That doesn't mean that they're unimportant.

While some actions (e.g. demanding that a woman on a train drop her book and headphones so she can be hit on) are minuscule in immediate consequence, they are indicative of a mentality that has already dismissed women's personal sovereignty, human dignity, or status as persons. They are not "that bad" in and of themselves, except that tolerating them supports the view that disregarding women's humanity is fine as long as the consequences aren't "that bad."

This approach leaves the creeps in charge. Unless they are challenged, they will take their behaviors precisely as far as they can without any consideration for the well-being of the women they are bothering. Some creeps may be the sexual equivalent of muggers and some "just" aggressive panhandlers, but none of them are people we want to be setting our boundaries for us.

There is more. Some predators test us with little things to see what kind of target we'd make. Will we be meek and quiet while they do their thing, or shriek like banshees and scratch out their corneas? Will we complain afterwards and get them duly punished, or be so ashamed of what happened to us that we'll let them get away with it? Will our community support us, or wave away any issues we raise just as they are waving away our concerns now? Tolerance for minor transgressions doesn't always translate into tolerance for major crimes, but it is a useful indicator. By putting up with little misbehaviors, we may put ourselves at risk of worse ones.

RECAP

Creeps are people who **consciously** behave in a manner likely to give someone an unpleasant feeling of fear or unease, specifically where there is a sexual undercurrent to that discomfort.

Negligent Creeps creep people out consciously but not deliberately. The discomfort is a by-product of their selfish attention-seeking behavior.

Malignant Creeps are low-level sexual predators who creep people out consciously and deliberately. The discomfort they cause is their goal.

A creep's behavior and the creeped-out feelings that behavior causes are his only distinguishing features. However, a creeped-out feeling can be caused accidentally.

The reason creeping is so ubiquitous is that it is a low-risk endeavor. Creeps hide in social situations. In many cultures there are vast gray areas between what is considered appropriate behavior and what is punished. Creeps deliberately play with those gray areas. They might deviate from the norm in ways that are hard to pinpoint or prove, or might have established a socially awkward persona in order to give themselves permission to behave inappropriately.

Creeps can be found in all groups and environments. However, in order for them to do their creeping, they have to find a space where:
- They can reliably find their targets of choice.
- They can creep without repercussions.

Some spaces and groups can become creep havens, in particularly if:
1. They allow normally inappropriate touching.
2. They value tolerance above all else.
3. They pride themselves on being special, separate from the mainstream.
4. They pride themselves on being the sort of places where that kind of thing just doesn't happen.

All types of creeping, regardless of the seriousness of individual transgressions, are the outward manifestations of a mentality that dismisses women's personal sovereignty. If the creeps are left unchallenged, many will escalate their activities to just as much as they can get away with. If we want them to respect normal, healthy boundaries, we will have to set and enforce those boundaries.

In order to learn to deal with creeps, we first need to learn about them: how they function, what attracts them, and what they thrive on. Once we've understood them, deterring them is a relatively simple task.

WHAT? SO WHAT? NOW WHAT?

One of the powers the creeps have is to make our brains go around in circles, never coming to a conclusion. They might take up a tiny proportion of our lives, yet end up occupying a disproportionate amount of our thoughts.

I use a trick to stop myself fantasizing over worst-case scenarios and to slam the brakes on circular thinking. When I catch myself over-reacting to an event, or thinking in spirals, I ask myself the following questions: what, so what, and now what.

- **What?**

What actually happened? Describe the event as it happened, in a purely factual fashion, without guesswork, embroidery, judgment, or rationalization. When we cut out all the chatter around the actual event, we might find it is not as problematic as we first thought.

- **So what?**

What is the fallout of the event? If there are no consequences, does the event matter?

- **Now what?**

Is there anything that needs to get done as a result of the event? If there is, do it. If there is not, set it aside and be done with it. It is unnecessary baggage.

This book will follow the same structure to disentangle the creep issue. We will start by looking at how we can gather and articulate facts about our issue. We will then go through the decision-making process that can help us choose the best course of action. We will end by looking at some of the actions we can take and how to evaluate their effectiveness.

(This technique is derived from Terry Borton's process of reflection.[4] However, I learnt it from reading Cosmopolitan at the dentist.)

---

[4] "Reach, Touch and Teach" by Terry Borton.

WHAT?

"If you deny reality you can't control reality."
– Rory Miller

DON'T DENY IT'S HAPPENING

One of the worst aspects of being the target of a creep is that it can be very hard to determine what the problem is, or even that there definitely is a problem. Working out exactly what is wrong and why can be so difficult that some targets can't even explain the problem to themselves. There is nothing tangible going on, just icky feelings and not-quite-right non-events. That puts us in a very uncertain situation, and human beings tend to dislike uncertainty. In order to avoid that uncertainty, we often bury those unpleasant feelings and try to convince ourselves that that there is nothing going on.

This isn't always the result of a conscious choice. Young women often are (or used to be – I'm getting older every day) culturally conditioned to ignore their own feelings for the sake of politeness. We are taught to force ourselves to ignore if something feels "wrong" in a social setting. Someone may say or do something that makes us feel uncomfortable, or push their boundaries beyond what we feel is acceptable, and our first duty is to not show it, not make a scene, not be rude. We suppress the feeling of wrongness and carry on being polite, until something happens that's bad enough to justify us taking action. Until then, we use tons of stock justifications to wave our discomfort away, ranging from denying that the behavior could be intentional to denying that it even took place. We try to convince ourselves that we must have got it wrong. That is **gaslighting**, pure and simple, and just because we're doing it to ourselves it doesn't make it OK.

Something happened, and now we feel creeped out. That is a fact. We might not know why. We might not know if our feeling is an emergency call from our intuition or a mental fart. However, **we know we feel creeped out. We must not deny that is happening.**

"Do not deny it's happening" is one of Peyton Quinn's Rules for de-escalating social violence. Denial not only doesn't make the problem go away, but it can make it worse, for two reasons.

First of all, once we start lying to ourselves about that kind of sensation we are gagging our intuition- our ability to know without knowing why.[5] Although our intuition can be corrupted by a number of factors – past experiences, cultural indoctrination, prejudices, etc. – there is no upside to shutting it up. By ignoring our intuition we can fail to read critical

---

[5] "The Gift of Fear "by Gavin de Becker.

signs, which can put us in serious danger. By paying attention to it – not necessarily acting upon it right away, but acknowledging its messages, investigating them further, and working out what caused them – we can help improve both our intuition and our ability to interpret it. This is not about letting vague feelings lead us blindly by the nose; it's about learning to pay attention to our intuition and to let it inform our decision-making.

Secondly, if we decide to bury our intuition, to silence it to prevent it from sending those unpleasant feelings our way, we can end up looking for the wrong kind of evidence. Once we decide that everything is hunky dory, confirmation bias, the tendency to favor information that confirms our preconceptions, will make us look for evidence that everything is OK and ignore any evidence that things are not OK. Creeps are masters at putting out confusing evidence. By focusing on the positive and ignoring the negative, we're actively helping them fool us.

This combination of denial and confirmation bias pretty much destroys our chances of being able to work out what our problem is, let alone to articulate it. How can we assess a situation when we're refusing to look at it? How can we gather evidence to help us articulate our problem when we're so busy proving to ourselves that the problem doesn't exist?

Sometimes we give ourselves seemingly very good reasons for ignoring our uncomfortable feelings: mustn't judge, can't jump to conclusions, give them the benefit of the doubt, innocent until proven guilty. Although our intentions here may be good, this point of view is not only nonsensical, but counterproductive and potentially dangerous.

What we are saying is that people's feelings are important and need to be protected... unless they are *our* feelings. What does that make us? Lesser people? Non-people?

Cultural conditioning plays a huge part in this. We are taught from childhood to disregard our feelings in order to protect other people's. We are taught that it's OK for people to make us feel uncomfortable, repulsed, or even threatened, and in return it is our duty to make them feel good about themselves and not to rock the boat. We are taught to ignore the subtle signals and to let wrong things progress far too far. We are taught to play by social scripts regardless of where they lead us.

Cultural conditioning also has us so wrapped up in how we do justice at a societal level that we try to replicate the process in our own heads. Our concept of justice is a deeply-held belief; it's so deeply-held, in fact, that many or even most of us don't even see it as a belief. Many western legal concepts – burden of proof, innocent until proven guilty, innocent by reason of insanity, *mens rea*, the need for an unbiased jury, the value of precedent, etc. – have become internalized beliefs for most of us. *Of course* someone is innocent until proven guilty. *Of course* it matters whether people hurt us or purpose or by accident. *Of course* everyone should be equal under the law. *Of course* we can't hold people who are in a mentally unbalanced state to the same standards.

I'm not saying that the underpinnings of our legal system are wrong. I'm saying that we have to be aware that they are beliefs. They are not facts. They are not the only way to do business. The Vikings, the Mongols, the Klingons, would laugh their heads off at them, and at us for believing in them. More importantly, our legal processes are designed to work at a societal level. They require a set of resources that an individual simply doesn't have. For instance, after a robbery a police department may start an investigation. This may involve trained investigators, forensic experts, witnesses, psychologists, substance abuse specialists, and legal counselors. The balance of evidence will be looked at by twelve uninvolved individuals. A legal expert will act on their conclusions, based on law and precedent. If we are expecting to replicate that process in our own heads, we're being a tad unrealistic.

Most importantly, our legal system is designed to work after the fact. It doesn't work at preventing crime. It isn't and never was designed to do that. It's designed to allocate proper punishment after something has happened. And, as individuals, punishing perpetrators may be something we don't have the ability or the right to do.

When we are faced with someone we are not sure about, who gives us an uneasy feeling, who makes our intuition tingle, we may not have the time and resources to play police-forensics-lawyer-witness-jury before taking steps. That's not a problem, though, because we don't have to play judge either. We don't have to play any part of that game. There are plenty of steps we can take that are not punitive steps.

First of all, though, we have to realize that our negative feelings towards something or someone are not punitive. When we find ourselves made uncomfortable by something someone is doing, that discomfort is not inherently a value judgment on that something or that someone. All we are saying is that we don't like it. That's neither an insult nor is it something up for argument: our feelings are facts, and we are not required to justify or defend them.

The decisions we make based on those feelings are also not punitive. As adults we have the right to manage our comfort level. We do not have a duty to like everything and we have the right to say "no" to what we don't like. That doesn't mean that we are punishing the things we don't like. If we do not want to eat oysters because we think they are slimy, we can say no to them. We are not punishing the oysters or the people involved in their preparation: we are simply saying no to something we don't like.

If anyone tries to foist the oysters upon us, by whatever means, then it is they who are trespassing against us. They are committing a **consent violation** by ignoring our stated "no." The fact that the matter at hand is not sexual doesn't make it less of a consent violation; if anything, it should be an indication to us that we absolutely do not want to find ourselves in a sexual setting with that person.

The same criteria that apply to snot-textured food apply to people's behavior. If instead of not wanting an oyster we don't want a hug: the same principles apply. When we say "no" to something we do not like, we are not punishing that behavior: we are simply managing our own comfort level.

We have the right to set conditions on what we want to do and how we want to do it. If someone doesn't respect our preferences, we have the right to manage our comfort levels by managing our exposure to that person. That is not a punishment we are visiting on them. Hardly anyone has an intrinsic right to our time, and nobody has an *unconditional* right to our time. Our time and attention are not a natural resource we're obliged to bestow upon all who ask; they are ours to allocate any way we like.

In order to get to that stage, though, we first have to cast off the notion that acknowledging our negative feelings towards something or someone is A Bad Thing – that our feelings, on their own, can hurt other people.

No feeling is wrong. No feeling ought to be disallowed. We have the right to our feelings. They may be a sign of our intuition kicking off, a symptom of our paranoia, or anything in between, but they are there and they are real. Denying our feelings is unlikely to make them go away; on the contrary, it's more likely to make them pop out unexpectedly and uncontrollably at inconvenient moments.

Not denying that something is happening is essential to our ability to handle pretty much any kind of situation. Not letting anyone else deny that it's happening is equally important. Nobody has the right to deny our feelings. They may not agree with them, they may believe that there is no valid reason for us to feel them, and they may not be willing to go along with them. However, they do not have the right to deny their existence or demand that we do.

OBSERVATION AND ARTICULATION

Once we have accepted that something or someone is making us feel uneasy, **provided that we are in a physically safe situation** we can turn our attention to what exactly is giving us that feeling.

*Note: if you are in a physically unsafe situation – for instance, if you are alone with a creep, if you can't get help quickly, if you are outnumbered, or if the creep has gone physical or has threatened to go physical – that's not the time to worry about information gathering. That is the time to **get the hell out**. If someone tries to prevent you from leaving the situation, that is a clear indication that you are in danger. In many jurisdictions that person is already committing the crime of unlawful detention and/or false imprisonment. They are depriving you of your bodily autonomy, and people who do that are not safe to be around. Get out by any means necessary.*

We met this guy Kasey, and we feel creeped out by him. But what *exactly* about Kasey is causing that feeling? Working out the precise reason that our spidey-sense started tingling can help us both address the situation and articulate it to others.

We may realize that what is bothering us isn't what Kasey is doing, but what he is. In particular, we may discover that the problem is a reflection of our past history or prejudices. Kasey is wearing the same cologne as our pervy high-school PE teacher. Kasey's rhinitis makes his breathing sound like that of an obscene caller who used to bother us before caller ID was a thing. Kasey has the wrong skin color, the wrong clothes, the wrong haircut, or the wrong accent, and our grandma always warned us against "those people." It's embarrassing to admit that our intuition is affected by prejudice, but that's the only way we can move past it.

Alternatively, we may realize that something about Kasey's behavior really is bothering us. That doesn't mean that his behavior is inherently inappropriate, though. In order to determine that, we need to be familiar with the behavioral code of that particular place and subculture. We need to know what's normal to recognize what is not.

If it turns out that Kasey's behavior is locally normal and what we want falls outside the local norms, that doesn't necessarily mean that we have to shut up and put up. However, it should inform how we go about asking for a behavioral change. That's when words like "please" come handy.

If there's a mismatch between an aspect of Kasey's behavior and what is normal/safe/pleasant/appropriate, we can continue our observations so we can work out exactly what it is. The more specific we can be, the better.

Paying attention to the details of Kasey's behavior makes us able to articulate our observations. In turn, articulating our observations can help us notice more things. Observation and articulation feed into each other and are useful skills to practice and develop.

Much of the time, though, when we observe creeps what we notice may seem insignificant: so what if Kasey stands a little bit too close? So what if his hugs are too tight? Continued observation and articulation, however, may help us notice patterns in Kasey's (mis)behavior. Over time, it could enable us to build a case against him. At the very least, it will help us connect more closely with our intuition. We will learn to use it with more finesse, and in doing so we will train it to inform us more clearly about the problems we are facing.

Red flags

The creeping game takes place in the gray areas between behavior that is deemed acceptable and behavior that is punished.

Behavioral codes vary wildly between groups and in different settings, and are always changing. Behaviors fall in and out of fashion. Pinching a secretary's derrière was acceptable a hundred years ago, tolerated 50 years ago, and is now illegal – here, at least. Somewhere else, it may be illegal but tolerated, or legal and frowned upon, or perfectly OK.

As a result, there is no universality to what behavior classes as "creepy." There are, however, universal red flags – behaviors that indicate reliably that a person is creeping. As cultures and behavioral codes change, that may change, too, but in this time and place there are five **red flags** that can be used to reliably identify a creep:

1. The creepy behavior is targeted.

Targeted behavior doesn't happen by accident. Someone who has a genuine problem with personal space, for instance, will stand too close to everybody. They won't just do it when they're around women and definitely not just when they're around a specific woman.

2. The creepy behavior can be turned on and off at will.

If someone can behave when there is a chance he will be swallowing his own teeth if he doesn't, then he is choosing not to behave the rest of the time. For instance, someone who has filters when the guys are around but descends into filth and smut as soon as they are out the door isn't someone with a behavioral problem; he is, at a minimum, an asshole.

Incidentally, this is why men don't tend to see creeps as often as women do: the creeps are scared of them. Creeps either go hunting where it's safer, or turn their behavior on and off. As a result, even though all members of a social group know an individual, only the women may experience his creepy side.

3. The behavior is preceded by an apology.

Someone who tells us ahead of time that he is going to be behaving inappropriately towards us is seeking our **permission** to do so. He is grooming us to be his victim by getting us to tolerate the inappropriate behavior.

This isn't the same as someone warning us that they have a problem so we can hash it out together. For instance, someone who knows that their filters aren't great may tell us that they know they have this problem, and if they overstep their boundaries to please tell them so they can curb their behavior. That doesn't even come close to someone telling us that they have no filters so they will be telling us inappropriate things, and "sorry" but that's just how it's going to be. The former is taking steps to reduce the chances of causing us discomfort. The latter is grooming us into accepting behavior that they know is inappropriate.

4. The behavior is accompanied by mock-apologies.

A good apology is more than a vague "sorry" thrown in our general direction. A good apology will include three things: an expression of regret, the assumption of responsibility, and a suggestion for a remedy. The following examples are *not* apologies:

- "I am sorry but..." Every word before the "but" can safely be ignored.
- "I am sorry if..." The "if" casts doubt on the reality of our experience.
- "I am sorry if I came across as a creep." "I am sorry if you thought I was a creep." Not only does the "if" cast doubt on the whole thing, but the person is not even apologizing for the upset they caused us. They are apologizing for damaging their own image.
- Apologies that do not contain a promise that the behavior will not happen again are nothing but excuses.
- Apologies given while the unacceptable behavior is being carried out are demands for our permission to allow the behavior to continue.

People who give us a mock-apology are not at all sorry. They are operating under the assumption that an apology will be enough to force us to tolerate the behavior. They are exploiting our politeness.

Lastly, an apology should not assume that forgiveness will be forthcoming. That is entirely up to the injured party, not to the person who injured them. It also should not imply that normal social relations will resume. We can forgive someone and still not want them around.

5. The behavior is allegedly a problem, but in reality it brings benefits.

A problem is something that brings difficulties to the person affected by it. Whatever it is – a disability, a psychological or emotional issue, a personality defect, a failure in upbringing – it doesn't make the life of the affected person easier. It might not make their existence a living hell, but it doesn't bring a net positive to their lives.

People who justify their bad behavior with a label and demand that those around them tolerate it, regardless of its fallout, don't have a problem; they have an excuse. They are using that label so they don't have to change their behavior. People who really have a problem and are trying to deal with it will be sincerely apologetic, not self-righteous, and will not seek to benefit from that problem. They will be asking for our forgiveness and actively trying to make changes, not demanding our forbearance so they can carry on getting away with misbehaving.

Through careful observation, we might start to notice patterns. For instance, we may notice that Kasey's behavior, although accidental-looking, is actually targeted. Kasey might stand too close to everyone... but he stands closer to the women than to the men. Kasey is forever in people's way... but he backs the hell out when the men ask him to, while he forces the women to squeeze past him. Kasey might hug everyone... but his hands only stray too low when he's hugging women. Kasey may shake hands with the men and hug the women... but he A-frame hugs women over a certain age, while he squishes himself against younger women so that their entire bodies are touching. Kasey may say inappropriate things to all the women... except to those who would scream bloody murder, or lump him in the face with a chair.

These red flags are not only useful in identifying creeps, but are also easy to articulate to third parties. If we can point out the inconsistencies in Kasey's behavior, we can get over a major hurdle in recruiting support: we may be experiencing a side of Kasey that nobody else is seeing, not because he's a poor innocent guy but because he is deliberately selecting which people witness his inappropriate behavior. That indicates that his behavior is intentional – if it was unintentional, he would be doing that with everyone, all the time.

If the behavior is challenged, perhaps several times, and met with consistent pushback on the part of the person carrying it out, that is a red flag of a different kind. An inability or unwillingness to change may be the result of a conscious choice, or the symptom of an underlying problem or personality trait the person in question genuinely has no control over. Regardless of the underlying cause, the person knows that their behavior is bothering people and they are not able or willing to change it. This suggests that further polite requests will have no impact on their future behavior. Rather than have a negotiation about our conflicting needs, we are likely to have an actual conflict.

This is particularly likely to be the case when the person in question continues to experience the same problems and still blames his problems on everyone but himself; for instance, if he is always "unfairly accused" or "women always exaggerate." He might not be lying: he might genuinely believe that the issue is with everyone but him. That makes him the social equivalent of the old joke:

A guy is driving home from work when his wife phones him.

"Honey," she says in a worried voice, "be careful. There was a bit on the news just now. Someone is driving the wrong way down the freeway!"

"It's worse than that," he replies. "There are hundreds of them!"

On "Socially Awkward"

Creeping behavior can mask really well. If it didn't, it wouldn't be creeping: it'd be sexual harassment or sexual assault and get punished accordingly. Even when we can pinpoint what exactly about the behavior is not-quite-right, we may not have any idea as to whether it is intentional. What if that guy doesn't mean anything by that? What if he is just socially awkward?

The key word here is "just:" once someone is labeled as "socially awkward," the assumption tends to be that all our problems with him stem from his social awkwardness. We get so focused on screening for people who make us feel uncomfortable by accident that we forget that personal attributes aren't necessarily mutually exclusive.

Someone can be socially awkward *and* a predator, or a bully, or a misogynist, or any other awful thing we may think of. The "just" in "just socially awkward" is not a given.

Let's say that we're trying to find out whether someone is "just" socially awkward, or deliberately being mean. There are two parameters here:

- Do they have "normal" social skills? Do they know how to interact "normally" with people? Do they know what makes people feel comfortable or uncomfortable? Can they read "normal" interpersonal cues?
- Do they get a kick out of hurting people?

Someone can have social skills and enjoy hurting people (i.e. a socialized sociopath). Someone can have no social skills and be a lovely person (i.e. the stereotypical unfortunate person with a heart of gold but an inability to make or retain friends). Someone can have social skills and be a lovely person (e.g. Mary Poppins). Someone can have no social skills and be a horrible person (e.g. the stereotypical misfit who ends up in prison for doing something horrific).

If we're looking at two factors, unless those two factors are mutually exclusive that gives us four possible combinations. The more factors we are looking at, the more combinations are possible. If we fail to consider the possibility of certain combinations, we can end up entirely misinterpreting some people's actions; we can end up attributing their motivations to one single factor when several are actually in play. Worse than that, we can end up excusing their behavior because they are affected by one negative attribute, poor things, while actually they're presenting a whole host of issues, some of which may be malignant.

For instance, those gamer guys who spout rape and death threats against women gamers may well be extremely socially awkward, but they're also criminals, because they are breaking our laws; they are also misogynists, based on their words; they are also bullies, trying to intimidate those they believe to be weaker than them; they are also cowards, preferring to do their intimidation anonymously; they are also giant flaming assholes. They are not "just" socially awkward. And their social awkwardness may be the least of anyone's worries.

Ultimately, it shouldn't matter whether someone is socially awkward or not. If we find a behavior problematic, for whatever reason, we have the right to take steps not to be exposed to it. Socially awkward people do not inherently get an exemption from that.

The only real difference between "normal" and "socially awkward" people is that when dealing with the latter we will need to be very clear in how we express our problem. We cannot rely on body language or tone of voice. We cannot skirt around saying "no": vague responses like "...maybe some other time" may be taken literally time and time again. If we want to resolve the issue, we will need to use our words to clearly express what our problem is and what changes we would like to see.

RECAP

We can't start to get a grip with any problem if we deny that it exists. When we feel creeped out by someone, we have to admit that the feeling is there. That doesn't mean that we have to act on it.

If we are in a physically safe situation, we can take the time to **observe** the person who is creeping us out and pinpoint what exactly about them we find uncomfortable. Is it a personal trait? Is it a behavior? Careful observations will enable us to **articulate** the problem, both to ourselves and to third parties.

An effective creep's game is so subtle that what we observe will be nothing more than a collection of minute deviations from "normal" behavior; if it wasn't, the inappropriate behavior would be obvious and potentially punished. As a result, each individual bit of misbehavior may sound insignificant on its own. However, when we put them all together, a pattern may start to emerge.

It can be very hard to determine whether we are dealing with a creep or someone bothering us by accident unless we spot one of these **red flags**:

- The creepy behavior is targeted.
- The creepy behavior can be turned on and off at will.
- The behavior is preceded by an apology.
- The behavior is accompanied by mock-apologies.
- An alleged problem brings social benefits.

If the behavior is challenged, perhaps several times, and met with consistent pushbacks on the part of the person carrying it out, that is a red flag of a different kind. Polite requests are unlikely to help with the issues, and unless other steps are taken the behavior is likely to stay.

It can be hard to tell between a "socially awkward" person and a creep. Some creeps exploit that by creating a "socially awkward" persona to take advantage of people's kindness. Also, being socially awkward doesn't stop a person from being other things too.

Just because someone is socially awkward it doesn't mean that we can't ask them to manage certain behaviors around us if those behaviors make us uncomfortable.

We are not under any kind of obligation to like everything and everyone. We have a right to manage our comfort levels, and that includes saying "no" to anything we don't like. However, there are often consequences to doing so.

So What?

"It is much easier and safer to scare someone into submission than to beat them into submission."
– Rory Miller

...AND?

We have accepted that we are feeling creeped out by Kasey. As there is nothing physically dangerous about our situation, we have taken the time to observe his behavior in detail. We have managed to spot a number of ways in which his behavior deviates from the norm. Although no individual deviation is significant, when we put them all together they add up to a giant bag of creepy. The presence of a few red flags indicates that the creeping is not accidental, that Kasey is more than "just socially awkward." We've caught ourselves a creep.

So what?

Just because we have enough evidence that Kasey is a creep, it doesn't mean that we *must* take steps. We might *want* to take steps, absolutely, but we don't necessarily *have* to.

What is the likely fallout of our discovery? If there are no likely consequences, does Kasey's creep status matter? If he can't do anything to us or anyone else – and that includes making us feel bad through his behavior – is he a baddy we *have* to fight? Is he a baddy we *want* to fight? What do we want to get out of this?

If we decide to take steps, they should be the steps that take us in the direction we want to go, the result of a strategy designed to bring us closer to our goals. Being reactive, particularly if we are doing so without any kind of forethought, may not further our goals and could get us in trouble. I am not saying that we should not take action: I am saying that we should take the action we really want to take.

What we might not realize is that by doing what we have already done – giving ourselves permission to feel our creeped-out feelings, to observe and data-gather, to articulate our observation, even if only to ourselves – we have already taken action. We stepped off the creep's script and shone a light on his behavior. That, in and of itself, is the most important anti-creep action we can take.

I like to refer to creeps as **cock-roaches** (pun intended). They have much in common with their insect namesakes: they are repugnant, they can make a place unpleasant purely by being there, they rely on our inability to catch them in order to continue plaguing us, and *when we flip the light on them, they scuttle away*. Predators don't generally like being at the receiving end of calm, calculated observation. They want us confused and threatened, not focused and planning. By refusing to panic or gaslight ourselves, we are already foiling their game.

CREEPING IS A SCRIPT.

Rory Miller wrote about scripts in "Conflict Communications".[6] The subject is both important and extensive, but the crux of the matter is that:

"Your natural responses to conflict are subconscious, scripted, and for the good of the group."

When we are dealing with a creep we are in a conflict: what we want is at odds with what he wants. If we let ourselves fall into our natural response, we will default to whatever our creep script is and follow it unthinkingly to its routine end. That is what scripts do to us: unless we become aware of them and will ourselves to break free from them, they automate our responses. We will do what we've always done and get what we always got, even though we don't like any part of it.

The most common creep script is also the worst one for us and the best one for the creep. It's a four-part skit:

1. The creep does something that makes us feel creeped out. An expert creep will do precisely as much as it takes to achieve that result, and nothing more.
2. We get caught in a vortex, torn between our negative feelings and our social conditioning. Our feelings want us to stomp on the creepy creature with all our might or run off shrieking. Our social conditioning dictates that we must be nice, not upset anyone, not misbehave, not make a scene. The normal result of these conflicting impulses is a horrified inaction laced with fear and disgust.
3. A malignant creep will harvest that fear and disgust to get a sense of power. A negligent creep will simply benefit from our freeze; it gives him the opportunity to take up our time and attention.
4. The creep uses that interaction to learn about us, so he can fine-tune his script to make it even creepier.

And then we do it all over again.

This response is subconscious. We don't rationally choose it.

This response is scripted. We find ourselves stuck going along with it, and we experience a feeling of wrongness if we try to derail it.

This response is for the good of the group. In the short term, it doesn't rock the boat. In the long term, it may damage the group as a whole, because women are likely to leave, but our socio-emotional brains aren't terribly good at long-term planning.

---

[6] "Conflict Communications: A New Paradigm in Conscious Communication" by Rory Miller.

Potentially, that script can run indefinitely, with us feeling like crap and the creep getting his jollies. As situations go, it is beautifully stable and relatively safe. The only problem is that it sucks. Not only does it detract from our lives, but it gives the creep what he wants. Unless we derail the script, the creep is going to be coming back for more.

So what do we do?

In a very real sense, we've already taken the first, biggest step. When we chose to believe our intuition, to engage our observation, to start working on our articulation, we stepped off that script. By stopping ourselves from falling into that vortex, from allowing the creep to confuse us into inaction and fear, we have already scuppered his plans.

Some creeps will give up there and then. They came to us hoping to get a specific reaction, hoping to be in control while we panic and freeze. Instead they got put under a magnifying glass by a concerned but unfazed observer. That's not the response they looked for and it's unlikely to get them what they want.

Any response other than the expected one pushes the script off the rails. Give the creeps anything but fear, freezing, and compliance. We only need to do that a few times, sometimes just the once, and most creeps are just going to disappear.

Maybe our creep is the persistent, stubborn sort, or just so well-established in our group that he won't be deterred so easily. In that case, we might want to take further steps.

I can't tell you what those steps should be. Neither can anyone else. Anyone who tells you they can is lying to you, unless they know you personally and very well.

I could give you some generic, one-size-fits-all guff, but your best option forward will depend on all kinds of factors: who the creep is, your relative position of power, your status in your group, the kind of group you're in, your personality, and, first and foremost, what you want to get out of this. If all you want is to get rid of the creep and you aren't concerned about any kind of social repercussion, you can be direct even to the point of harshness. In other situations, that may not be your best bet. But provided you do anything other than follow the script, you're going to improve your position.

GOALS

Before we decide on a course of action, we need to work out what we want to achieve. We are unlikely to get what we want if we don't even know what that is.

When dealing with creeps, we may have all kinds of different goals:

- I want to be everyone's favorite person, whatever the cost.
- I want to be a proper lady.
- I want to get on well with most of the people around me, but I want them to respect my boundaries.
- I want to remain a member of this group.
- I want to understand the creeper's motivations.
- I want to feel comfortable, not creeped out.
- I want to protect myself.
- I want to protect other group members.
- I want to stop the problem from escalating.
- I want all creeping to stop everywhere in the world.
- I want to teach that fucking creep a lesson.

We need to be clear about what goals we want to achieve, particularly as some are not compatible. We are unlikely to be able to carry out a bloody revenge on our creep *and* retain our image as the sweetest gal in the office. We are unlikely to be able to raise the issue of entrenched creepdom in our group *and* not make a fuss. Most of the time we will need to decide what we want the most, and accept that we won't be able to get everything.

The rule of thumb for goals is that they need to be **S.M.A.R.T.**:

Specific: the goal needs to be adequately defined. We want Kasey to stop standing so close to us vs. We want Kasey to stop being such a creep.

Measurable: we need to have a parameter establishing when the goal is accomplished. We want Kasey to stand at least at arm's length from us at all times vs. We want him not to crowd us.

Achievable: the goal has to be achievable given our constraints and limitations. We want Kasey to stand further away from us vs. We want to shoot him into hyperspace with a catapult.

Relevant: the goal has to meet our needs. Getting Kasey to stand further away from us would make his presence less creepy. Getting him to learn to play the kazoo, not so much.

Time bound: we may not be able to set a deadline for when the change will take place as that's not just up to us, but we can set a deadline for when we will act. The best time for that is usually "as soon as we have gathered the relevant resources."

The "achievable" part of the goal is particularly important. It isn't just about whether a goal is theoretically possible, but about whether we are willing to do the work necessary to bringing it about and to pay the relevant costs. It may be conceptually possible to get our creeping CEO fired or to have his activities severely curtailed, but we may not be in a position to bring that about. Alternatively, it may be possible for us to do it, but too costly, because he pays our wages and we need the money. That doesn't make us wimps or hypocrites; it just makes us pragmatic. Not everyone can lay everything on the altar of the cause. People have responsibilities and limitations. Wanting something and being unwilling or unable to pay the cost is an entirely distinct issue from wanting something and not being willing to work for it. Provided that we don't lie to ourselves about our situation and the motivations behind our decisions, we will usually be able to find a compromise between what we ideally want and what we can actually achieve.

Working towards an achievable goal is infinitely more productive than failing to work towards an unachievable one: even if we only get half of what we really want, at least we're getting somewhere.

The depth of our game will hinge on what our goal is. Do we just want to manage our comfort level? Do we want to change the creeper into someone or something else? Do we want to change the culture of the entire workplace?

We are allowed to change our goals as we go. For instance, we may start small, just wanting to be left the hell alone to enjoy our hobby in peace, but once we achieve that we might discover that it's not enough for us, that we do not want to fight every incoming creep individually, that what we want is a change in what our group tolerates. We may do the opposite: start out with a lofty goal, determine that it's too much effort, or too costly, and scale it down to whatever makes our immediate problem go away. If we change our goals we should make sure that they are still S.M.A.R.T., and our strategy and tactics should change accordingly.

Resources and costs

In order to evaluate whether our goals are **achievable** we need to work out what resources it will take us to get there. In order to evaluate whether our goals are **worth achieving**, we need to work out what it will cost us if we succeed or fail. Do we have the resources to support our endeavors? Are we willing to pay the price?

In an ideal world, the only important factor in determining the result of a conflict would be who is right and who is wrong. In this case, Kasey is behaving inappropriately, which is all kinds of messed up, and we just want not to be creeped out, which is perfectly fair. Ergo, we should "win" this conflict without even trying.

Unfortunately we don't live in an ideal world. If we choose to bring our conflict of interest with Kasey out in the open, all kinds of factors are going to have an impact on whether we are successful or not and how much our efforts cost us. If this conflict is taking place in a social or professional setting, social or professional factors will bear the most weight, including:

- Our respective positions in the group's hierarchy.
- Our reputations.
- The self-identity and core values of the group; in particular, if these contribute to it being a creep haven.
- How conflict-averse the group is.

For extremely conflict-averse people, the mere fact that we brought the conflict up can be enough to make the whole thing our fault. For them, whoever mentions a problem is the cause of the problem. This makes no sense and is completely unfair, but it is the standard operating procedure in all kinds of toxic environments, from abusive families to dysfunctional workplaces.

The offence will be seen as particularly serious if the conflict involves a protected person within the group – someone who enjoys a special status due to their personal attributes or their history with the group. Is Kasey the Grand Master of our martial arts club, or the Bishop of our church? Is he a poor unfortunate soul that every other group had cast aside and we gathered to our bosom, proving our superior righteousness? Is he just useful? Is he the guy who is horrible to girls but is a wiz at writing code or fixing cars? Is he the only dude with a table big enough for us to play Risk on, or the only one able to buy beer with his fake ID? Does he have tenure?

This kind of unfairness may benefit us if we are more useful, have a solid reputation, or if we were here first. The group may side with us for reasons that have nothing to do with the conflict per se, but grant us a "win" nonetheless.

That is one of the most interesting (or horrifying) aspects of dealing with creeps: in this type of conflict our social group can be a resource, a cost, or a bit of both.

Enlisting the help of our friends and associates works as a force multiplier. More people on our side means more people keeping an eye out for trouble, more people ready to respond if an inappropriate behavior occurs, more witnesses to back our version of the story. Communication works as a light on the creep: once we warn other people of his game, he will find it much harder to misbehave unseen and unchallenged.

...provided that our social group is aware of creeps and their behavior, supporting of our boundaries, and willing to either let us enforce them or to step in and ensure that they are respected. Unfortunately, that isn't always the case.

VICTIM BLAMING

People's reactions to a problem are often far more influenced by how the problem affect their belief system than by what is actually going on. If a problem clashes with their beliefs, they will often subconsciously prefer to warp facts in their mind rather than have their beliefs shaken.

There are people out there who believe that women who "misbehave" by acting "inappropriately" deserve the trouble they get. In our mainstream culture that kind of victim blaming is increasingly considered an aberration, but it hasn't gone extinct yet. In other cultures, unfortunately, it is still the norm.[7]

When we tell them that we've experienced some creeping, victim blamers won't support us. They may also elect to further punish us by judging, isolating, or even shunning us. Since their blaming is a consequence of a deeply-held belief, they are very unlikely to change.

Some people totally disagree with victim blaming, yet engage in behaviors that are so similar as to be indistinguishable. This is particularly true of people who go their entire lives without encountering a sex predator or sex pest. Over time, they subconsciously convince themselves that "bad things don't happen to good people," or "that sort of thing just doesn't happen around here." They end up creating and living in an

---

[7] TRIGGER WARNING: SEXUAL VIOLENCE. http://www.independent.co.uk/news/world/asia/delhi-bus-rapist-blames-dead-victim-for-attack-because-girls-are-responsible-for-rape-10079894.html

imaginary safety bubble.

When somebody in their circle has a bad experience, they struggle to process that fact. Admitting that their lifestyle doesn't grant them total safety would burst their safety bubble. Selfish as this sounds, their subconscious priority is the preservation of their illusory feeling of safety.

If we go to them with our creeping problem, they will most likely launch a personal inquisition to find out what we did wrong – because, from their naïve point of view, we *must* have done something wrong for something bad to happen. We must have been in the wrong place, done the wrong things, given out the wrong signals, wore the wrong clothes, etc. By finding out what we did wrong, they can work out the moral of the story and turn the event into a cautionary tale. They can then convince themselves that avoiding certain behaviors will guarantee their safety. While this interpretation of the events is intended solely to preserve their sense of safety, the result is still a form of victim blaming.

Their reaction can be even more extreme if the problem hits close to home, metaphorically or literally; if the creep is someone close to them. Unable to deal with the fact that their social network includes unsavory individuals, they will either avoid being around us altogether or demand that we pretend that nothing ever happened. While we are a living reminder that they lives are not as safe as they desperately want them to be, they will not tolerate our presence.

If we are unfortunate enough to have one or more of this kind of person in our lives, we are likely to find ourselves at the receiving end of all manner of shoddy behaviors – inquisitions, judging, blaming, isolation, etc. – and *none of them will have anything to do with us*. These behaviors, however painful, are solely people's attempts at processing our problem without having to readjust their mental compass. No matter how personal it may all feel, it is not. It's totally about them, not us. We need to remind ourselves of that fact, because they won't be able to see it, let alone admit to it.

Victim blaming can be even harder to deal with when we are doing it to ourselves. Self-blaming can be the result of our own beliefs or the internalizing of other people's voices. Our internal voices are impossible to avoid and can be even harder to silence than the external ones.

If we find ourselves losing perspective, it may help to think of how we would treat a loved one experiencing the same problem. Would we concentrate on accusing them or supporting them? We should show ourselves the same care, kindness, and consideration that we show those we love.

LEVELS OF VIOLENCE

Being willing and able to stand up for what is right in a firm but polite manner doesn't always make us respected and popular. As explained by Rory Miller in "Violence: A Writer's Guide," the problem stems from the fact that people operate at different levels of violence – which isn't just the use of physical force, but any type of force used to resolve a situation. The levels are:

- Nice: people who avoid conflict.
- Manipulators: people willing to use underhanded, covert social tactics to get what they want.
- Assertive: people willing to speak out and set boundaries; i.e. willing to engage in open, direct confrontation.
- Aggressive: people willing to resort to verbal violence – swearing, screaming, and threatening.
- Assaultive: people willing to resort to physical violence.
- Murderous: people willing to kill.

The problem isn't just that different people operate at different levels, but that some people cannot comprehend the motivations and beliefs of people operating at a different level from them. As Miller states:

> "At each level, the people who use the level feel fully justified... and they universally characterize the people below them as weak and the people above them as bad."

What that means in practice is that if we are surrounded mostly by nice people and we act assertively, they may see us as bullies, even if we are acting out of necessity and using our powers for good. They will judge us not based on our goals or our achievements, but on the means we are willing to use to get there.

Furthermore, by speaking out we may also be undermining the structure of our group. We are changing things, and people tend to be frightened of change, even when they hate what they have at the moment. This is particularly significant if the group is close-knit or long-established. Our great-uncle may be a huge creep, but if we are willing to stand up to him we should be prepared to say goodbye to harmonious family Christmases.

COST-BENEFIT ANALYSIS

Ultimately, what we need to ask ourselves is whether it is worth it. Is opening a conflict against this particular person worth the hassle that it will cause us? What would be the cost of inaction?

Working out the cost-benefit analysis of a particular interaction doesn't mean that we need to sit down and draw a graph in each and every moment, but it does mean that we should think about the fallout of doing and not doing certain things. This is linked to our goals: are they realistic? We may be hypothetically willing to carry out an action, but are we willing to pay the resulting costs?

There are many aspects of a situation to consider when deciding whether engaging is worth it or not:

- What do we stand to lose?
- What do we stand to gain?
- How much hassle will the conflict be, regardless of how it ends? How much time, energy, and money will it suck out of us?
- What are the chances of retaliation?
- What kind of relationship do we have with the person in question, and how much will the conflict impact our social network?

The last question is probably the most important in determining whether to engage or not and how far to go. There is a huge difference between standing up to someone who is a part of our life, someone we can't avoid, and to a perfect stranger we may never meet again. By standing up to a person in our life we are setting boundaries that can benefit us over time. Although in the short-term things may be difficult, in the long-term those boundaries will hopefully make our life better.

Standing up to a stranger over a minor transgression that isn't escalating is unlikely to bring the same positive results to our life. The societal impact, however, could potentially be significant. If we encourage more women to stand up by modeling assertive boundary setting behavior, we could slowly but surely change the environment we live in.

The costs of our actions will also vary depending on our connection with the creep in question. If we expose a stranger for creeping in a public place, we potentially put ourselves at risk of immediate physical retaliation, but the longer-term social costs of our action are likely to be negligible. If we expose a member of our social circle, the opposite may be the case: we may be safe from violent repercussions, but the social fallout of our allegation is likely to hit us hard. The closer we are to him, the harder our actions are likely to impact our social group. Even though we are in the right, even though we may win, even though our social group may support us through it all, we are still likely to suffer some consequences.

If we are normal-ish people with normal-ish backgrounds and normal-ish social lives, we will be aware of and attached to our social capital and the benefits it brings us. Even if we never consciously think about it, chances are that it will be a factor influencing our decisions. Most of the time, there's nothing wrong with that. That's how we get to be functional members of a social group: by giving a damn about other people and behaving accordingly. Our problems start when we can't switch that mechanism off in the face of dangerous situations. If someone is trying to assault us, that's not the time to worry about how grandma said that "hands are not for hitting." But to switch that mechanism off altogether, to ignore what our social group deems appropriate for the sake of "winning" conflicts, regardless of the stakes, can cost us dearly.

When we are running a cost-benefit analysis, we should give equal consideration to the costs of doing a thing and the costs of not doing that thing, or doing nothing. For instance, if we expose our great-uncle for creeping, we might create a huge rift in our family. If we don't, we allow all of our family members, children included, to be the targets of creeping behavior and perhaps worse.

It is essential to establish ahead of time how far we are willing to go and what we are willing to tolerate. As well as giving us the chance to pre-emptively gather the resources we need to minimize the cost of our actions, it will free up thinking time in the moment and may shorten our freeze: we won't be stuck trying to resolve an internal conflict, because we have already resolved it.

Deciding that we don't care about the fallout and we just want to fight creepdom in all its aspects, at any cost, is a valid outcome of a cost-benefit analysis. We just need to make sure that it is a reasoned decision, not a knee-jerk reaction.

MINIMIZING THE COST OF STANDING UP

There are three main concerns that stop women from standing up against creeps:
- Escalation or retaliation on the creep's part.
- Getting it wrong and treating an innocent person as a creep.
- Social repercussions, either for just standing up or for getting it wrong.

There is an ongoing push in the self-defense world to educate women as to how unreasonable the first concern is. Statistical and anecdotal evidence suggests that the chances of being assaulted for simply turning someone's unwanted sexual advances down are minimal. The stories circulated by sites such as "When Women Refuse"[8] are, if not sensationalistic, at least outliers: they are extreme occurrences that, because of their shocking nature, end up taking up a disproportionate amount of public attention. The argument is that women shouldn't allow this kind of event to unduly affect their views on the subject. This argument is valid, to a certain extent, but it rather misses the point.

Many if not most women *know* that there is a non-zero chance of men reacting badly to rejection. This isn't something we fear because our poor little bunny brains are so prone to flights of fancy: we actually *know* it, because it has happened to us, around us, or to women we know. Maybe we have never seen the kind of extreme violence that makes the news, but many of us have seen men turn to verbal abuse, insults, slurs, low-level stalking, professional sabotage, bullying, shouting, threatening behaviors, vandalism, and sometimes to physical violence. Our concerns derive from personal or shared experiences of being at the receiving end of various levels of aggression, not from the lurid reportage of one-in-a-million violent events.

How likely that aggression is to turn to violence will depend on a lot of factors, first and foremost our environment; in some subcultures responding to a perceived insult with violence is the norm, while in others it's something you only hear about in the news.

The fact that this risk is a reality is going to affect how we approach the issue, regardless of how low a chance it has. Even though the vast majority of women who turn down a creep do not end up with a black eye, the fact that a black eye is possible will affect how we approach that situation. There is nothing wrong with that: knowing that something could result in violence and willfully ignoring that fact is just shoddy self-defense.

Awareness of a low-chance risk doesn't have to result in avoidance of anything and everything that could bring that risk about. We can keep both facts in mind: the possibility of things going south, and the relatively low chance of them doing so. Good risk assessments include both the identification of what the hazards are (e.g., being physically assaulted) and an assessment of their chance of coming about. A non-zero risk is a risk. That doesn't have to paralyze us into inaction, particularly as that risk does not exist in a vacuum.

The risk that doesn't get nearly as much media attention is the risk of not speaking up, of allowing situations to escalate until they reach a point

---

[8] TRIGGER WARNING: VIOLENCE, SEXUAL VIOLENCE. There is also a very real chance of becoming very depressed about humanity at large. http://whenwomenrefuse.tumblr.com/

where we *have* to act. Situations that start badly hardly ever improve of their own accord. The guy who is pushy about buying us a drink is unlikely to be less pushy about following us out of the bar. If he responds badly to the first rejection, he's unlikely to respond any better to the second, bigger one: the more invested he is, the more hopeful he is of getting somewhere with us, the more his behavior is likely to stray from what is acceptable. There's always a risk of escalation and retaliation when deciding to shut someone down. That risk may be high, low, or utterly unpredictable. However, the risk of escalation is usually greater if we don't nip a situation in the bud.

If direct confrontation feels like the wrong answer, getting the hell out of there as quietly and as safely as possible may be the best option. This is a strategy that a large proportion of women tend to naturally select for the simple reason that *it works*. When standing up is too risky and not doing anything even more so, getting the hell out of Dodge can get us home safe. Alas, this strategy is regularly derided for not being assertive enough or inherently resulting in a "loss," either for individuals or for Womanhood. Yes, by leaving a bar rather than challenging a creep we are not defending our personal right or Women's right to be there undisturbed, and we are doing nothing to ensure that the creep gets his just deserts; however, we are also not risking our front teeth in a confrontation. And if we stay in that bar even though we don't feel safe because it's our right to do so, are we going to have a good night out, anyway? It is up to each one of us to assess our particular situation and pick the solution that best meets our needs. Armchair quarterbacks are welcome to make different choices when their turn comes up.

The other two concerns – mistaking an innocent person for a creep and being socially punished for standing up – are linked and often stem from the same issue: the way in which women are socialized to deal with conflict.

There is no universality to women's socialization: it is ever-changing, as well as being different in different subcultures. However, we can generalize some trends throughout our culture. One of them is that women tend to be socialized without any middle gears.

I mentioned Rory Miller's classification of the levels of violence: nice – manipulative – assertive – aggressive – assaultive – murderous.[9] Women

---

[9] "Violence: A Writer's Guide" by Rory Miller.

in our culture have traditionally been raised to be nice or manipulative in "normal" everyday interactions. Assertiveness is the mark of a "bossy bitch." Assertiveness towards males is still seen in some corners as a direct affront to their manhood. Women who are socialized in this manner tend to respond to worsening conflict by staying nice or manipulative until it is obvious that these strategies have failed, that the situation is no longer physically safe… and then they flip out and maul somebody.

As strategies go, this has its merits: the element of surprise can work extremely well in an assault, though it does nothing to prevent it. As a strategy for dealing with social conflict, however, it's fairly disastrous. What we're essentially doing is not giving anyone any inkling that there is a problem – not the person with whom we have the problem, and definitely not any onlookers – and then, out of the blue, going berserk. We may be able to articulate our way out of this, to explain exactly what caused our reaction and why it was justified, but it is likely to be a tough sell. Even if we were totally in the right – if our assessment of the creep status of a person was 100% accurate and if his misbehavior warranted a stern response – the way in which we reacted is likely to make people assume that we are at least part of the problem.

In most environments, if assertiveness makes us "bitches," going off at someone for no reason whatsoever makes us "crazy bitches." That reputation may serve us or damages us depending on our environment, but it may not be something we want to court.

Many women fear doing anything because they fear doing too much, yet they increase their chance of needing to do too much by doing nothing. It's a vicious circle that can only be broken by taking prompt, justified, appropriate action early on in a situation. In most situations, that "action" need be nothing more than telling someone that something doesn't sit well with us. We don't want them to hug us. We don't want them to buy us a drink. We don't want them to use our work email to romance us. And we don't need to smash a chair on their head to convey this.

Some dedicated women's self-defense courses exacerbate this problem. Almost all of the physical skills they teach are at the assaultive/murderous end of the spectrum, and the only thing that's taught lower down is a generic "just say 'no'" that doesn't provide any useful guidance to people who aren't used to being assertive. If our social conditioning has left us without middle gears, self-defense training that reinforces that gap will not help us.

We need to expand our view of suitable conflict management options, to practice using lower-end methods and escalate gradually if necessary.

Learning to say a clear "no" before we bellow a "fuck off and die" is difficult for many of us, but it's the best way out of this bind.

Learning to use our middle gears and to articulate what we did and why lowers our risk of social repercussions in response to a conflict. We need to be able to explain to the people we want in our corner what the problem was *and* how we tried to resolve it amicably. An amicable resolution may not be in the cards, but our attempt at securing one will bolster our position. We are creating a context for any future action, so that if we choose to escalate we won't be doing so in a vacuum.

Furthermore, the amicable resolution could work out, and if it does it won't matter whether our initial assessment was right. We were addressing a behavior and managing our comfort level, not making a diagnosis or meting out punishments. If we use our words to express to someone calmly and clearly that he's making us feel uncomfortable and he stops his behavior, it won't matter whether he was "really" a creep or "just" socially awkward. Our request got us a result without causing any damage to anyone or anything. For many of us, that is the best result we can hope for.

CREEPS VS. ALLIES

An experienced creep can single-handedly wreck a social group, or at the very least shake its members' trust in the group's cohesion and ability to function. Most often the split takes place along gender lines.

The women, who may have been targets of the creep in question or have learned through previous experience how creeps operate, want the creep removed from the group or his behavior controlled. The men don't get it. They may have never been exposed to the worst of the creep's misbehavior because he was clever enough to behave himself while they were watching. They may have no previous experience in dealing with sexual predators, so they may not understand how they operate. The bottom line is that not only don't the men go all blood-thirsty berserker on the creep, but they may try to sweep his misbehavior under the rug. As a result, the creep is often allowed to stay and continue with his creeping. Women may leave the group as a result, while the creep endures, protected by his supporters.

This is often hailed as an example of rape culture – of prevailing social attitudes that normalize or trivialize sexual assault and harassment. It doesn't have to be, though. Other factors may play a role:

1. The social rift is part of the creep's strategy.

Predatory behavior often requires that a predator cut off the chosen prey from the herd. That isolation doesn't have to be physical. If a creep creates a rift in a social group, that can increase his chances to pester his target undeterred. If the predator is playing a psychological game and wishes to terrify the target, stripping her of her social network is an effective strategy.

Some creeps are very good actors, able to behave in wildly different ways depending on who is watching. If a creep has a solid reputation built over a period of time, people may find it hard to believe us when we try to expose him, particularly if we have no proof. This is a difficult situation to navigate both for the target and for the group.

2. The ability to deal with creeps isn't gender-related.

Dealing with creeps is awkward. It isn't just awkward for women; it is awkward all round. The sense of uncertainty and confusion that creeps can create is not gender-specific.

Guys may find it difficult to deal with this type of situation precisely for the same reason we do: because they lack the necessary knowledge, skills, and confidence. They may feel as powerless as we do to deal with this kind of underhanded strategy. They may be as concerned as we are about making a bad call and unnecessarily hurting someone's feelings, about being socially shamed for their actions, about possible escalation or retaliation. They may be just as scared as we are, just not as comfortable admitting it to themselves, to the world, and particularly to the women who are asking them to step up and help. Gender expectations dictate that guys should naturally know how to fix this (and everything else). Our requests for help can make them feel pressured and inadequate, thereby reducing their ability to function.

Modern social trends don't help them either. It is very common for the male allies of women to be accused of being "white knights," of being overly defensive of women in a desperate attempt to get laid. They are accused of "virtue signaling," of taking conspicuous but useless actions ostensibly to support a good cause but actually just to show off their superior character. They are accused of being sexist: if they truly believe that women are equal to men, why do they step up so readily to defend them?

All of these accusations have their places, but most of them are thrown about purely to shut male allies up and deprive women of a valuable resource. White knights are out there, and they are a problem women need to learn to guard against; but to suppose that the *only* possible reason for a man to care about women is to get laid says more about the person launching that accusation than about the reality of the situation. Virtue signaling is also a thing, but it is not necessarily a bad thing. It definitely beats the "iniquity signaling" that plenty of people engage in by defending men's right to objectify, mistreat, marginalize, or even abuse women. Men speaking out against men who treat women poorly can have a positive effect, even if they don't do anything else. The positive effect can be disproportionate, in fact, and greater than that of women speaking out.

A study conducted on Twitter[10] on anti-black racism, status, and race showed that direct, negative responses to racist tweets can have an impact on reducing that behavior, but the impact depends on who sends those tweets. Interventions by higher-status white users have the greatest positive response, while interventions by low-status white users and black users do not achieve much. This should come as no surprise: racist people don't value the opinion of the people affected by their racism, and will respond best to same-race people in positions of authority. The latter part is just a common human trait, and the former is inherent to the issue.

Although I am not aware of the same kind of study having been conducted with regards to misogyny and sexism, anecdotal evidence abounds. Men who don't respect women, who regard them as inherently inferior, will not respect their opinions and preferences. They might, however, respond well to men in authority who call them out on their behavior. This makes the actions of male allies incredibly important, both with regard to individual instances and to society-wide issues. If more men in position of authority stepped forward to condemn low-level sexual predation, we may see a society-wide shift in the right direction. The opposite is also true: a man in a position of authority who encourages other men to objectify or harass women can have a disproportionately negative impact on the problem as a whole.

As for the accusations of sexism – that if a man speaks out for women then he is inherently treating them as inferiors – it is so asinine that it's hard to disentangle it. Quite simply, people do not only speak out to protect their inferiors; that assumption is ludicrous and speaks volumes about the persons making it. Men and women can speak out against a problem because it affects a fellow human being and they care; gender and relative power don't have to come into it. The people who can't realize this can't see past their own sexism.

---

[10] https://arstechnica.co.uk/science/2016/11/twitter-bots-can-reduce-racist-slurs-if-people-think-the-bots-are-white/

3. Imprecise articulation leads to misunderstandings.

A creep's actions often differ only slightly from those of a well-intentioned, regular guy. They are designed specifically for that purpose: to closely mimic normal social interactions in order to avoid repercussions.

This can make our articulation very difficult. It can be hard to express how those minute deviations from the norm can be so upsetting. If we cannot explain our issues to the rest of the people in our group, they may not understand what we are on about. This difficulty is one of the reasons creeps so often thrive.

Inaccurate articulation can damage our cause, particularly when:

- Our descriptions are so vague that all the men in the group feel personally accused. If we describe the creep's actions without specifying exactly how they deviate from the norm, or how they happen in a specific pattern, other guys may believe that we are tarring them with the same brush. They do that too, so are we accusing them of being creeps? They will end up justifying the behavior to absolve themselves, and absolve the creep in the process.

- We skip descriptions altogether and run straight to name-calling and blaming. Particularly in the heat of the moment, it's easy to slip into this mode of speech. However, unless we provide clear, solid evidence that backs our assertions, all we have done is launched an assault on a person. There is a world of difference between acknowledging our feelings and apportioning blame, between saying "I feel creeped out by Kasey" and "Kasey is a creep." The first is a statement of fact, however vague, while the second is an accusation. If Kasey is at all popular, people may be moved instinctively to defend him, and may spend more efforts in proving us wrong than in listening to what we have to say.

The best way to articulate our issue is to present a list of objective, observable events, rather than rely on people accepting our interpretation of the situation. "Kasey keeps standing too close to me" is very different from "Kasey makes me feel creeped out." People can actually see that Kasey is standing too close, but they can't see how we feel.

If we have spotted any red flags, we can use them to point out that the behavior is unlikely to be accidental. "Have you noticed how Kasey always stands too close to the girls, but never to the guys?" Even if people do not believe us then and there, because they didn't notice any such thing, by making them aware of that pattern we make it easier to spot.

Being specific about behaviors and patterns also helps us open people's eyes to a creep's strategy. If our "Kasey keeps standing too close to me" is met with "but he doesn't do it with me!" or "he's never done that in front of me!" that can be used to highlight the fact that his behavior is targeted, hence very unlikely to be innocent.

4. We plead for help rather than ask for it.

I have lost count of the number of times I've heard women describe how they tried to get the men in their lives – friends, relatives, even their partner – to help them with a creep problem and got zip. In fact, not only they didn't get any kind of support, but said men continued to befriend the creep, and sometimes asked them to do the same.

This kind of situation infuriates me and I would not attempt to justify it. It does, however, show a recurring pattern: those women ask for help and, when the help is denied, do nothing. They don't dump the creep-friendly partner. They continue to hang out with the creep-friendly friends. For the men in question, there is no cost whatsoever to siding with the creep. Those requests are thrown out there in the hope that they will result in a positive reaction, but with nothing to back them up. There are no consequences to ignoring them.

The help and support of the people in our social network is not an optional extra, a boon they may or may not grant us: it is an essential part of any functional, healthy relationship. If our loved ones don't want to support us in a difficult situation, that is not OK. And if our loved ones attempt to convince us to continue to stay in the difficult situation, to continue befriending a person who is making us deeply uncomfortable and may wish us harm, that is a whole new level of messed up, and the only correct answer is NO.

The next chapter will look at boundary setting techniques. These are not creep-specific: we can use them with our loved ones, too. Standing up to the people who (allegedly) love us can be hard, but it is good practice for standing up to those who hate us.

When it comes to creeps, we need to remind ourselves and the people in our lives that neutrality is a myth. With social issues, inaction is equivalent to support for whoever has the upper hand in a given moment. The objectification of women is still rampant in our society, and creepy behavior is one of its manifestations. Those guys who are proud to state that they see both sides of the issue, that they trust women's ability to navigate it alone, or that it's simply none of their business are not being neutral: their apathy actively supports the creeps.

TACTICS AND STRATEGY

Once we have established our goals and checked that they are S.M.A.R.T., we need to decide what we are actually going to do to reach them. We need to work out both our tactics and our strategy —what we are going to do in the moment and what our overall plan is for achieving what we want. The two should be matched. If our tactics aren't going to bring forward our strategy, if our means don't lead to our end, we need to readjust either or both parameters until they do.

Establishing our goals, our strategy, and our tactics reduces our chance of getting sucked into unfocused or knee-jerk actions that may or may not help our cause. It can also stop us rationalizing our actions after the fact. If we carry out actions that are unlikely to lead us towards our goal, we cannot use that goal in order to justify them.

Resource gathering and maintenance should be a part of our strategy. It is utterly useless to try to pull off tactics and strategies if we lack the resources to do so. A lot of that resource-gathering will be in the social realm; we might try to enlist the support, or at least the awareness, of the people around us. We may also wish to gather a broader range of resources: to improve our personal safety, to take a public speaking class, to discuss our concerns with a friend or even a therapist. Anything that makes us better able to deal with our issue is a resource and a step in the right direction.

If you can't do anything, do something.

None of us is utterly powerless. There is always something we can do. Small deeds accumulate. By doing what we can do as well as we can, we can move, however slightly or slowly, towards our goal. The only actions that can't have a good impact are the ones we don't carry out.

Above all, we should focus on actual *doing*, rather than fantasize about it. We may have grand ideas about what we would do if only, or what we will do one day, but those fantasies have no impact on our actual lives. The tiniest action we actually carry out has an infinitely greater impact than any glorious action we never get around to.

It's easy to undermine our own efforts. We may say that something addresses only the symptoms, not the root issues, or that it addresses the issues in the long-term, but does nothing to help here and now. These criticisms may be accurate, but they are not constructive. Personally, I'm going to get pain meds *and* get my broken bones set, not one or the other. I take the same approach to dealing with social issues.

RECAP

Just because we've identified a creep, it doesn't mean that we have to do something about him. If there is no fallout to our discovery, we might decide to do nothing. However, chances are that by engaging in our identification process we have already done something.

Rory Miller wrote that "natural responses to conflict are subconscious, scripted, and for the good of the group." The most common creep script is also the one that most benefits the creep: the creep puts the creeping in, and we respond by falling into a cognitive freeze that grants him our attention, our time, and our negative feelings.

By refusing to follow the creep script we are already taking action against him: we are thwarting his intentions and denying him what he wants. Many creeps will give up on us at that point, purely because creeping us out is too much like hard work.

We may decide to take further action. That decision should be based on our goals. We need to establish our goals if we want to have any hope of achieving them, and they should be S.M.A.R.T. goals.

Once we have established our goals, we need to run a cost-benefit analysis. Is opening a conflict against this particular creep worth the hassle that it will cause us? Are we willing to pay the cost? What would be the cost of inaction? The likely costs and benefits will vary hugely depending on whether the creep is a stranger versus a person close to us.

In this context, our social group can be a resource, a potential cost, or a bit of both. This will depend on the nature of our social group, on the creep's position within it, and on how we handle the conflict.

Aside from escalation or retaliation on the creep's part, the most likely costs of standing up are social. The fear of antagonizing our social group is what stops a lot of us from standing up. We can minimize that risk by learning to operate at different levels of conflict, so we can escalate gradually if the conflict escalates, rather than letting the situation degenerate. Gradual escalation and precise articulation are essential to ensuring that our social group supports us through this process.

The role of male allies in dealing with individual creeps and with creeping at a societal level is particularly important. Precise articulation can help cultivate a supportive group of male allies.

Some individuals will fail to support us not because of anything we are doing or not doing, but because they are victim blamers. Their attitude is a reflection of their beliefs and mental processes, not of the events in question, and definitely not of us.

NOW WHAT?

"*You teach people how to treat you by what you allow, what you stop, and what you reinforce.*"
– *Tony Gaskins*

Do the thing

Strategies are perfectly useless if we don't act upon them. Once we have assessed the situation and run a cost-benefit analysis of whether it's worthwhile for us to do anything about it, there comes the time for action.

The two most useful options generally are:

- If there is anything we need to get done, get it done.
- If there isn't anything we need to get done, set the event aside. We do not need to spend any more time fretting about it.

Both options might sound like they are more easily said than done, and they are. However, we have already spent a considerable amount of time thinking about the pros and cons of our options. Unless we want to turn our strategic planning into rumination, the next step is taking action, even if that action is deliberately doing nothing and moving on.

GOING OFF-SCRIPT

We have decided that we need to take action, that we have to address the issue. Based on our observations, we may have a pretty good idea that we are dealing with a creep, but we can't be sure. Based on our cost-benefit analysis, we're fairly optimistic that the cost of standing up won't outweigh the benefits, but we can't really know without trying. We have done what we can to ensure that our social group won't ostracize us as a result, but we can't be totally sure about that either.

This would all be very daunting if we needed to throw ourselves into this conflict with our metaphorical guns blazing. Fortunately, we don't. All we have to do is stop the creeping, which is a behavior that works on a script. The creeping is made possible by our adherence to the script. All we have to do is deviate from that script, stop playing our part according to the rules, and it will all fall apart.

As far as the standard creep script goes, near enough any change is an improvement. How we deviate from the script is immaterial, provided that our response isn't what the creep wants. As long as what we give out isn't the expected response of freeze, fear, and horrified confusion, pretty much anything goes.

Chances are that some responses will come more naturally to us than others, depending on our personality and inclinations. I tend to fall into either being full of glee, because the fates have sent me someone I can hurt without feeling bad about it, or studying the creep in question like a bug under a microscope. Apparently they don't like that at all. Those are just my go-to responses, though. It pays to go for what feels natural and comfortable, what actually works for us rather than what we think should work; anything that gets the creep off our back is the right response.

The only exceptions are responses that break one of Peyton Quinn's Five Rules for not escalating social violence. I mentioned one earlier, "do not deny it's happening." These are the remaining four:

- Do not insult him.
- Do not challenge him.
- Do not threaten him.
- Give him a face saving exit.

If the response we select breaks one or more of these rules, there is a chance that the creep in question will feel obliged to escalate. The likelihood of that happening depends on the creep's background and inclination rather than on ours, so to be on the safe side it is better to avoid that kind of response.

I class derailing the script as a destructive response. It's easy (once you get used to it) and it can be a lot of fun, but it works better at putting creeps off than at teaching them to treat us right. It also won't help socially awkward people who are creeping us out by accident.

If we want to be constructive with our response, we will have to use our words to express our problem and set our boundaries. It's nowhere near as much fun as showing a creep on the train the picture of a freshly dissected human liver in our forensics book,[11] pretending to talk to his invisible friend, or reciting "Green Eggs and Ham," but it is more beneficial in establishing a new relationship with creeps we can't get rid of. It also stops the onlookers from wondering about our mental health. Some people are no fun at all.

Talking about the problem with the creep in question is also essential if we decide to take further steps against him or to bring the problem to the authorities. The first thing they are likely to ask us is whether we have tried to resolve the issue ourselves, and talking to the creep about it is an essential step in that process.

---

[11] That happened. It was a fun moment. I do not encourage you to carry dissected liver photographs for that purpose, unless that's what you enjoy.

BOUNDARY SETTING

One of the rules of thumb about managing difficult people is that we will probably need to establish boundaries with them. Boundary setting allows us to prevent their difficult behavior from affecting us; effectively, we are retraining the difficult people to behave "properly" around us.

The stages of boundary setting are:

- **Set**. We decide what the boundary is going to be.
- **Ask**. We clearly request something, such as a change in behavior.
- **Tell**. We reiterate our request more firmly and present the consequences of not respecting it. Boundary setting without consequences is just begging.
- **Consequences.** We do exactly as we said we would do.

This process works with anyone capable of understanding it – our boss, our parents, our children, the greengrocer who stares at our boobs, and so on. The basic process is precisely the same, though the way we manifest our wishes and the consequences we set may be very different.

All these steps have to be followed. If we miss any of them out or repeat a step more than once, the process won't work. Repeating a request time and time again and doing nothing about it teaches people that our words can be ignored.

SETTING OUR BOUNDARY

Earlier we spoke about goal setting, and how we need to decide what our goals are before taking action or even making any plans for action. The same applies to boundary setting. We need to decide what it is that we want – normally a behavioral change. Our boundary, like our goal, needs to be S.M.A.R.T.:

Specific. Kasey won't touch our leg while we play D&D (or ever).

Measurable. Kasey's hand will not touch our leg.

Achievable. Kasey is capable of keeping his hands to himself. We are capable of moving away or leaving if he does not comply.

Relevant. Kasey not touching us will make his presence less unpleasant.

Time bound: The boundary starts the moment we tell Kasey, and will persist indefinitely.

Asking

We need to clearly request what we want. We cannot expect people to read our minds, or to know and agree to our standards of behavior. If we are incapable or unwilling to clearly request what we want or need, we need to work out why that is. Are we scared of the consequences? Are we already expecting the situation to end badly? Are we subconsciously aware that we are being unreasonable or unfair?

If we have an ominous feeling about starting the boundary setting process, it could just be that we are pushing ourselves out of our comfort zone. Doing something that is out of character is never comfortable until we become used to it, which takes practice. Alternatively, our feelings may be accurately telling us that we are starting something that is unlikely to go smoothly. Boundary setting is not always a comfortable process. Each situation is different, and only we can determine the source of our reticence.

The situation can be even trickier if we are dealing with someone who is genuinely socially awkward, rather than pretending in order to misbehave. There's a rule of thumb in dealing with truly socially awkward people: if we clearly and politely point out their social mistakes and tell them how to fix them, they will comply. If they do not comply, then either they are feigning social awkwardness for their own convenience, or they are not *just* socially awkward. We can therefore use the little lesson we gave them as a litmus test to determine whether they are people we may want to help along or people we can squish without compunction.

There's a tiny problem with this rule: it is extremely unreliable. It's a beautiful theory, but in real life it only tends to play out in very specific circumstances. It can work well when the person teaching the lesson is someone the socially awkward person respects and looks up to (merely being in a clear position of authority might not suffice; some socially awkward people have no innate respect for hierarchy). It can also work well with tourists. When someone is visiting a country where they don't know the rules, a local telling them that they're misbehaving may result in a genuine apology and a behavioral change. That is not a given, though: some tourists will have a hissy fit about foreigners and their backward ways instead. Even the people who do adjust their behavior may not do so out of an interest in doing the right thing: they might do so begrudgingly, forced by their politeness to indulge these benighted foreigners who don't know any better.

Outside of those two settings, I have never seen a person behaving in a socially awkward manner be told any permutation of "don't do X, it's not appropriate" and oblige. It doesn't matter what the underlying reasoning for the request was, whether it was about generic behavior ("that's grossly inappropriate"), the local environment ("we don't do it here"), or personal preferences ("I don't like it"). I have just never seen it work out.

I'm not saying that there are no people who are oblivious to non-verbal cues but respond well to specific requests, and who have been waiting all their lives for someone to explain things to them in a way they can parse. I have been told that they exist and I have no reason to doubt that. However, I have yet to encounter any of them out in the wild.

It makes sense, really: logical as the rule of thumb is, it doesn't explain how so many people get to grand old ages still being spectacularly socially awkward. Our society may be conflict-averse, but the chances of someone reaching pensionable age without ever having been told in a useful fashion that a behavior is obnoxious are minimal. That's the myth, though: that authentic socially awkward people will modify their behavior when given clear, specific instructions.

In real life, or at least in my real life, the responses I have seen are invariably one or more of the following:

- They tell me straight up that I'm wrong.
- They rule-lawyer me to death about why the behavior is OK either in general, or because they're doing it and they're pure of heart, so everything they do is by extension OK.
- They tell me that if I don't like someone doing X, I should engineer my environment so X can't be done around me. It's my fault if people are able to misbehave around me.
- They have a hissy fit and never speak to me again. I tend not to mourn their loss, but there can be consequences to this, particularly if they feel genuinely aggrieved by the cruelty I showed them.
- They tell me that they appreciate that the behavior is not OK, in general or for me, but they are going to carry on with it because it's not *that* bad, and they just don't want to give it up.
- They quit doing it around me, but they carry on with the same behavior somewhere else, where they think I can't see it.

The last two responses suggest that they could be creeps – negligent creeps in the former instance, quite possibly malignant creeps in the latter. The first four, however, don't tell me anything beyond the fact that if I want to see a change I will need to escalate, because asking nicely won't do it.

It is possible that every one of the people I've encountered in my misadventures has pretended to be socially awkward. I reckon that's not the case, though. I reckon that this theory is overly simplistic and doesn't take into account a rather important fact: that not everyone cares about everyone else's opinion.

Plenty of people don't care about what I know, think, or like. In their social hierarchy I'm a nonentity. I do not have the right to tell them what to do. I do not have the credibility to tell them that what they are doing is inappropriate. I am also not important enough to them to make them modify their behavior to suit me; to them, their convenience or sheer habit are more important than my preferences, and why shouldn't they be? Who am I to demand that they make changes? Aren't they just as entitled to ask me to change my requirements?

It's not just about me. I'm not that special. Those people react in a similar manner every time anyone they don't respect tries to get them to modify their behavior. That's how they got to be socially awkward at 30+, 40+, 50+: they discount information to the contrary. In umpteenth years' time, they will still be having the same conversations on the same subjects, and still wondering why they struggle so much to retain people in their lives.

This is important: if a man is a misogynist, or even just plain sexist, he will see *all women* as people who warrant no respect. Any time a woman asks him to modify his behavior, he will see that at best as an imposition, at worst as a challenge to his manhood. This response can easily turn into a feedback loop: a bad attitude towards women is manifested as ongoing bad behavior, which brings about negative reactions from women, which creates resentment towards women, which reinforces the bad attitude. Some guys who "can't talk to women" are just painfully shy, but not all of them are. Some of them are incurably sexist, unpleasant to be with, and sometimes downright dangerous. The modern trope of the "adorkable misogynist," who is viciously sexist but so far removed from typical masculinity that he's kinda cute with it, is whitewashing behaviors and attitudes that are dangerous to women.[12]

I do not mean to say that telling people clearly that we would like them to change their behavior never works; however, I think it's important for us to remember that it only tends to go smoothly when certain circumstances are in place. A lot of that hinges on the amount of personal power we wield. Are we big, strong and threatening? Are we well-connected? Are we high up in our organization? How much trouble could

---

[12] https://www.youtube.com/watch?time_continue=1255&v=X3-hOigoxHs

we cause the person whose behavior we want to modify?

The problem with this kind of process is that it can be difficult for us to establish why something works; the most we know is whether it worked or not. This is how many of those cookie-cutter, one-size-fits-all systems come about, and why they fail so many people.

Say that one of my 6' tall, 6' wide, multiple-black-belt-wearing, armed, male friends tells Kasey that a behavior is bothering him so could he cut it out, and Kasey complies. It could be that my friend has managed to help poor Kasey out by kindly explaining the rules of the world to him. It could be that he managed to find the precise formulation for expressing a request so it can't be ignored. It could be, however, that he has just unwittingly intimidated Kasey into compliance, and that the compliance will only last as long as my friend is around. My friend may have no idea *why* what he did worked, but the fact that he can make it work reliably may lead him to think that he has discovered The Ultimate System For Retraining People. The fact that for him the system works every time can make him believe that it is 100% effective. When I try to follow his system and don't get the same positive results, it might not occur to him that the problem may not be with my implementation; he doesn't know that some negotiations are just harder when you're a foot closer to the ground.

We need to remember that sometimes things will not work out for us because of the nature of the game, not because we are playing it badly. This is critical both for our strategy and for our sanity. Strategically, if something doesn't work for us, doing it harder may not be the best approach. We might be better served by seeking an alternative tool, one that fits us better. For our emotional welfare, the last thing we need is to punish ourselves for "failing" when all we've done is discovered that a tool doesn't work well for us.

The fact that asking might not work doesn't mean that we shouldn't try it. When asking works out for us, it could be all we need to do to solve our problem. Kasey may listen and the behavior may go away, just for the cost of us asking. We might still want to monitor his behavior to make sure that he hasn't just moved along to creep on another member of our group, or to another way of creeping, but we can consider this particular part of the problem resolved to our satisfaction.

Even when it doesn't solve our problem, asking is the pedestal upon which we can build the rest of our strategy. We have done what courtesy demands of us, and we can now move on.

A GENTLE SCRIPT FOR ASKING

There are countless ways of making the same request. Even if we express precisely the same content, we can totally change the message we are putting across by changing our tone and body language. I strongly suspect that most people who read this book aren't people who are happy to bellow threateningly in someone's face at the first offence, and if we err in any direction, it is going to be by being too gentle.

There is nothing inherently wrong with being gentle: starting gently gives us an opportunity to escalate if we need to. In many environments, it will also make us look more reasonable, and it will predispose people to side with us if we need to escalate. There is a social power to be gained by having a reputation as someone who is calm and polite: if we become agitated or rude people will assume that it's over something serious. There is also a social power to be gained by getting a reputation as the person who flips out at the slightest provocation, but that is a persona we may not be willing to embrace. However, there is no getting away from the need to be **clear** and **firm** in our requests. If we plead our requests, our very behavior suggests that complying with them is an optional extra.

My favorite way for gently and clearly expressing requests in a safe social setting is Dr. Marshall Rosenberg's **Nonviolent Communication (NVC)**.[13] NVC is often marketed as a cure-all for all types of conflicts, which it isn't. One of the main premises of NVC is that people have common needs, and our conflicts arise solely from the strategies we use in meeting those needs. Sharing our feelings and needs can show us how much we have in common, and help us find a mutually agreeable solution to our conflict. It would be lovely if that were true; unfortunately, it isn't. That premise rejects the existence of asocial conflict (more on that later), and as a result NVC is completely unprepared to deal with it.

When it comes to social conflict, however, NVC offers a very helpful script for navigating emotionally charged situations. This includes those situations in which *we* are the emotionally charged people, as well as those where there is a high risk of someone else getting emotionally charged.

NVC communication is based on a few concepts that sound mind-bogglingly obvious... until we realize that hardly anyone ever uses them. For instance, it's based on making sure that we actually understanding what the other person means before reacting. It's based on de-escalating ourselves first (though it doesn't use that expression – I stole that from

---

[13] "Nonviolent Communication: A Language of Life" by Dr. Marshall B. Rosenberg.

Rory Miller's "Conflict Communications"). It's based on fostering an internal dialogue that makes us better able to respect our emotions *and* to realize that they ultimately stem from how we are parsing our reality. It's based on communicating what we mean clearly, yet without antagonizing the people around us. Lastly, it is heavily scripted, which makes it suitable for those who are trying to learn a new way of interacting with those around them and want some clear, precise guidance.

Each request is composed of four parts:
- We express objectively what we observe.
- We express how that makes us feel.
- We express our need that is not being met.
- We request the change that would meet that need.

So, for instance, if we find Kasey creepifying because he stands too close, the script would go:

"Kasey, when I see you standing close enough to touch, I feel crowded out. Because I need more personal space to feel comfortable, would you be willing to step back so you are at arm's length, and stay there while we talk?"

Yes, it is long-winded, but it achieves several things:
- It makes the issue *our* issue. It's not an assault on the person we are talking to. Note the use of "I see" and "I feel" vs. "you do" and "you make me feel."
- It makes both the problem and the solution totally clear. This is particularly important if we are dealing with someone who genuinely doesn't get us: if they didn't even know they were causing us a problem until we told them, chances are they won't be able to immediately work out a solution unless we help them along a bit.
- It clearly states our requirements. Provided that those requirements are reasonable, if the person refuses to meet them or at least negotiate them, then we know that mere words won't help us here. If we want to see a change, we'll have to make it happen.

I love NVC because it's structured and reliable. Provided we don't mess with it, it won't mess with us. More than that, it gives us the opportunity to either solve the problem, or know for a fact that we are dealing with another type of problem altogether, which will require other solutions. The uncertainty is over. As far as I'm concerned, that's worth throwing a few extra words at a person.

There are other benefits, too:
- It makes us think before we react.
- By giving us a structured thinking process, NVC can help us break brain

freezes caused by uncertainty. We have something we can do, and while we're doing it we're not frozen.

- It can pull us out of emotional flashbacks. We can end up frozen by something entirely devoid of ill intent that reminds us of something painful in their past. NVC makes us work out the roots of our feelings, making us spot whether our reaction is to the present or the past. This can help us identify our own triggers for future work, as well as relate better to those who inadvertently trigger us.

- By making us describe what we observe objectively, without our interpretations or biases, it forces us to assess our own perceptions. We may discover that a situation or event was blown out of proportion by how we interpreted it. Conversely, we may discover that we were underplaying an issue.

- It forces us to own our emotional processes. Everything is framed in terms of "how I feel", not "how you are making me feel." Although the feeling may be a relatively direct result of someone's actions, the feeling is mine and mine alone. ("What others do may be a stimulus of our feelings, but not the cause."- Marshall B. Rosenberg.)

- It forces us to work out and admit our needs. Even if this remains purely an internal process, never vocalized, this is invaluable. People who do not know what they really need and people whose needs are unrealistic can hurt themselves and others trying to get their needs met. People who suppress their needs tend to live splendidly unhappy lives.

- It forces us to think about what changes need to be implemented in order to have our needs met. We may come to realize that the changes we require are unreasonable, or not practical. It is then up to us to work out a new strategy for handling the emotional impact of the situation.

In order to meet these criteria, NVC needs to be used as intended. Mangling the process can cause it to fail; that's no reflection on the process per se.

However, NVC is by no means perfect. In particular, it is not designed to deal with asocial conflict, as defined by Rory Miller.[14]

Asocial conflict and violence come from three levels on Maslow's Hierarchy of Needs:

- Survival: people operating out of the fear of immediate death (e.g. a drowning person fighting for air).

- Security: resource predators. They engage in conflict in order to get

---

[14] "Meditations on Violence: A Comparison of Martial Arts Training & Real World Violence" by Rory Miller.

stuff (e.g. a mugger).

- Self-actualization: process predators. They engage in conflict for their own pleasure (e.g. a rapist).

We could argue that these asocial problems still fit into the NVC model. However, we'd have to perform some serious mental gymnastics.

Drowning people do not care about whether we understand their feelings and needs; they just want air. If we are talking to them about how we empathize with their plight while we are throwing them a buoyancy aid, that's all good; but it's the buoyancy aid that's resolving their problem. If we physically engage with them, no amount of empathizing is going to prevent them from using us as a tool to get just one more breath of air. They're not in a mental space where our interpersonal connection matters. People suffering from certain mental illnesses or drug reactions can be in a very similar mental space.

Resource predators do not care about whether we understand their inner struggle; they just want our stuff. Following the NVC pattern may or may not work at keeping the situation relatively calm, depending on a variety of factors. Although it is certainly preferable to many other responses, it is risky. Ultimately, the conflict will not be resolved by how good a personal connection we manage to forge. Yes, there is a chance, however slim, that by humanizing ourselves we may change the nature of the situation... or we might get grievously injured, because we are nothing more than a sandwich wrapper that's stubbornly refusing to give up the sandwich.

Process predators may or may not care about our feelings and needs. If they do, that's not a good thing. Dealing with someone who actively enjoys our pain is hardly preferable to dealing with someone who just doesn't care about it. In this kind of situation, using the NVC model can make things infinitely worse. By admitting that our feelings are hurt, we are telling the predators that what they are doing is working. By stating our needs, we can make sure that they are never met. We are giving them helpful clues as to how to best injure us.

This sounds patently absurd if we think about people causing us physical harm: "When I see you sticking the screwdriver into my eyeball, I feel upset..." However, process predators don't operate only in these extreme settings. Physically torturing someone is a high-risk, often short-term game. Other forms of torture can be carried on indefinitely and without retribution. There are plenty of people out there who enjoy causing people emotional or psychological pain, knowing full well that they're likely to get away with it. Malignant creeps fit into this category.

If we use NVC techniques in asocial settings, which it isn't designed to deal with, they are very likely to fail. If they succeed, they will do so by accident.

The flipside of it is that we can use NVC to help us identify these settings. If someone takes delight in the suffering they are causing us, or consistently does not give a damn, then regardless of who they are, their roles in our lives, what they are doing, how they are doing it, etc., they are not safe people for us to be around. They don't have to be mad or bad; the fact that they're dangerous to know is enough of an issue.

NVC and any other verbal communication technique will only work if we can also regulate our non-verbal communication. We can't make someone believe that we are not scared while we are shaking and our voice is quivering. Managing our body is often much harder than controlling our words; however, it gets easier with practice. Practicing stating our requests in safe environments – with our friends or family, for instance – can help us build the skills and confidence to use the same techniques in environments that make us uncomfortable.

GIVE UP THE MIDDLE GROUND

One of the most dangerous myths in conflict management is that of the Middle Ground. The Middle Ground is a magical land which, once we reach it, will bring happiness and co-operation where grief and strife used to reign. "We were locked in this awful argument about this issue, but then we found the Middle Ground and *poof!* Everyone was happy!" The quantity of wishful thinking that goes into this is almost staggering.

First of all, if the middle ground was amenable to all, there wouldn't be a conflict in the first place. Conflicts don't occur just over misunderstandings. Sometimes people need or want incompatible things. In order to find a middle ground, everyone involved must be willing not just to negotiate (i.e. to talk about the issue), but also to compromise (i.e. to potentially settle for less than they need or want). Whenever that is not the case, the middle ground has to be fought for.

In fact, we may not have to fight just to gain it, but also to hold it. Unless everyone truly and willingly embraces the middle ground, the conflict will continue because disgruntled or disaffected people will continue pushing towards their original goal. This can be a particular problem when people feel righteous about their positions; even people who are willing to compromise on non-essential practical issues may fight to the last breath for what is Right. We are the same: would we compromise on issues like human trafficking or pedophilia?

Secondly, the middle ground approach hinges on the belief that everyone's position is reasonable, which is patently not always the case. Sometimes the middle ground is not a place we want to be. If someone wants to rape us, getting him to only stick it in half way is not an acceptable solution. There are plenty of less extreme situations when someone wants something we can't or won't accommodate. Giving in part way, while it may appease them in the short term, may not work for us.

Thirdly, giving in part way to someone's requests is not guaranteed to create a bond of friendship and respect; in fact, it can do precisely the opposite. No schoolyard bully ever became someone's friend because they gave up their lunches without a fight. The Danegeld did not make the Vikings like or respect the Anglo-Saxons. Essentially, if someone is trying to screw us and we give in part way, all we have achieved is showing them that we are willing to be screwed. The next time they will probably ask for more, because they know that the strategy works.

Telling and consequences

We have made our request to Kasey clearly, firmly, and politely. The behavior could be stopped with little or no inconvenience on Kasey's part. Yet, he chooses to carry it on. We now *know* that we are dealing with something more than an accidental faux pas.

Asking has failed. Asking again is unlikely to get us a different result and would undermine our credibility: very few people listen to broken records. We need to decide whether to escalate or give up.

Despite thousands of gung-ho memes to the contrary, **giving up is always an option**. It doesn't mean we've lost, or that we're betraying ourselves or the feminist ideal. We can quite simply come to the realization that it's just not worth it: what we could get out of "winning" isn't worth the time, effort, and stress that would go into securing that "victory." Instead of escalating, we can bail out.

If our main goal is to manage our comfort level and our happiness, and if we are happy to forego whatever it is that involves the creep in question, avoidance isn't losing: it's securing a victory for ourselves at the lowest possible cost. We just aren't that invested in joining Kasey's game of D&D, so we are going to spend our Thursday nights somewhere else.

Our avoidance doesn't necessarily undermine the progress of feminism, either, particularly when our money comes with us. We don't like it when the greengrocer openly stares at our boobs, so we will shop somewhere else. If women en masse stopped shopping anywhere where they're treated poorly, those shops would likely suffer.

In a very real sense, avoidance can be a way of imposing a consequence without going through the bother of all the intervening steps. If there is little or no cost to us doing so, nor any need on our part to educate the people we'll be avoiding, there is no reason why we shouldn't choose it.

Unfortunately, giving up is rarely cost-free, particularly in situations we can't or won't walk away from. We may not be able to quit our job or move house to avoid a creep; it may simply not be practical. We may also not be willing to curtail our social lives just to avoid dealing with an unpleasant person. We may want to continue playing D&D, even though Kasey is going to be there. Giving up on our boundaries in that setting could have negative consequences. If Kasey continues to touch our leg and we let him get away with it, we will teach him and anyone watching that they can ignore our requests and nobody cares, not even us. That is unlikely to improve the way we are treated.

Warning people of the incoming consequence is an essential part of this process. If we enforce consequences without having warned those at the receiving end, our behavior may well seem inexplicable, unjustified, and unfair. Instead of gaining a reputation as people who need to be respected, we may get one as people who lash out randomly. People may be more careful around us, but we are unlikely to gain friends or allies in the process, and we could lose some of the ones we already have.

We need to bear in mind that "presenting consequences" can be very similar to "making threats," which is a behavior that can escalate a situation. Part of it is about how we present the consequences, and part of it is about the person we're dealing with. Some people will take *any* attempt at presenting a consequence as a threat regardless of how it's presented, because that is how they roll. Many people, however, are sensitive to tone as much as content.

In order to push on with our boundary setting, we need to be able and willing to enforce the consequence in question. The term "consequence" has a rather unwarranted negative connotation in our culture, causing many of us to picture extreme or punitive behaviors. This doesn't have to be the case. A consequence doesn't have to be about us making something bad happen to the person in question (e.g. "If you touch my leg again, I will punch you in the face"). The consequence could be us removing something good (e.g. "If you touch my leg again, I will not sit next to you"). Whatever it is, it has to be something realistic. Threatening a ludicrous consequence diminishes our credibility.

ASSERTIVENESS

Assertiveness is often sold as a socially-approved cure-all for all kind of low-level problems. Unfortunately, that is not the case.

The effectiveness of assertiveness hinges on the social context in question. Assertiveness is designed to work between equals. If a person deemed to be inferior tries to be assertive with a superior, that person can get squashed, metaphorically or literally. Toddlers who are assertive with their parents don't gain a new level of respect within their family unit; they get a session on the naughty step. Pretty much the same dynamic is in operation if I (ostensibly female and tiny to boot) act assertively at someone who deems me inherently inferior (e.g. a misogynist). Who am I to talk to them like that?

Remember Peyton Quinn's Five Rules that, if broken, can escalate social violence?
- Don't deny it's happening.
- Do not insult him.
- Do not challenge him.
- Do not threaten him.
- Give him a face saving exit.

I can blow through the last four by assertively demanding a behavioral change from someone who deems me an inferior:
- I'm insulting them by treating them as my equal.
- I'm challenging them by demanding a change in their behavior.
- I'm threatening them by stating potential consequences.
- If I do the above in the presence of their peers, letting me get away with that kind of thing would bring about a public loss of face.

These issues are generally ignored when assertiveness is marketed and sold, possibly because it's unpopular to point out that, diversity statements notwithstanding, some people are still classed as subhuman by a proportion of the population. It is easier to insist that if we try to be assertive and fail, we must have been assertive wrong; that the failure of the process is our failure, not that of the tool we used. Not only does that mindset literally add insult to injury, but it is utterly counterproductive.

The push towards assertiveness may be aiming to overturn gender expectations for women, but it ignores how breaking those expectations can be punished. In many subcultures, women making a stand are behaving inappropriately, regardless of what they are standing up for. Even when men and women are supposed to play the same game – when they are in the same roles, expected to achieve the same results – they are supposed to play it with different rules and handicaps.

When a man asserts himself, he is an "alpha" or a "go-getter." People are impressed, because they have been conditioned to believe that men should be assertive. That is not how we are conditioned to believe women should behave. Women are supposed to be nice, to facilitate the smooth running of the group, be it a family or a corporation, even if that "smooth running" runs right over them and their rights as a human being. If a woman displays outward assertiveness, she is "bossy" or "a bitch."

The problem isn't when "the enemy" calls us bitches. The problem is when our people decide that we are bitches and treat us accordingly from then on. The problem is with having to choose between losing our social capital by being treated like a mat or by behaving in a way that is deemed gender-inappropriate. Due to societal expectations, we can find ourselves caught in lose-lose situations.

Assertiveness is a tool. If that tool doesn't work well for us, our short-term goals are better served by finding a tool that suits us than by scolding ourselves for not making it work. The important thing is to get the job done. Tools that don't get us closer to our goals are not useful.

ENFORCING CONSEQUENCES

If the need arises, we need to enforce the consequences we presented exactly as we presented them. Making empty threats or offering a discount on the consequences we promised will only make people discount our words in the future. For this reason, it is important to only threaten consequences that we can and will carry out.

Consequences need to be clear and impactful: a consequence that doesn't matter to the person being punished is a waste of effort on our part. Consequences do not have to be nasty, or even particularly antagonistic, though that is as much about presentation as about content. We can present them as the matter-of-fact result of a person's actions: "I said that if you kept touching my leg I would leave. You touched my leg, so now I'm leaving." "I asked you not to ring me. You rang me anyway, so I blocked your number."

If we do not have the means, rights, or opportunity to set clear and impactful consequences, boundaries setting will not work and could backfire. However, that is extremely unlikely. There is always *something* we can do to make the lives of the people around us a little bit more difficult, or a little bit less pleasant. If nothing else, we can generally remove ourselves from their immediate presence or their lives.

Operant conditioning

Skinner's **Operant Conditioning** is a method for obtaining behavioral changes via the application of consequences. It is based on the premise that behavior is influenced by the consequences that follow. In its bare bones it consists of **reinforcing good behavior and not reinforcing bad behavior**.

According to Skinner's model, a **punishment** is anything that causes the behavior to occur less often, while a **reinforcement** is anything that causes a behavior to occur more often.

Punishments can take two forms:
- Positive punishment: the addition of unfavorable consequences to a behavior which lead to a decrease in that behavior. For instance, every time Kasey touches our leg, we punch him in the nuts. The resulting testicular pain will demotivate Kasey from touching our leg, thereby weakening the behavior.
- Negative punishment or punishment by removal: the removal of a favorable consequence after a behavior occurs. For instance, every time Kasey touches our leg we get up and sit away from him, or we leave altogether. Assuming that Kasey enjoys our presence, removing ourselves in response to his behavior will result in a decrease in that behavior. (If Kasey doesn't enjoy our presence but everyone else does, our departure may result in him finding himself at the receiving end of positive punishment by everyone else.)

We can also attempt to modify Kasey's behavior via reinforcements – consequences that make the good behavior take place more often.

Reinforcements can take two forms:
- Positive reinforcers: favorable outcomes in response to good behavior. For instance, all the boys who don't stare at our breasts get a cupcake, or are invited to another activity we run.
- Negative reinforcers: the removal of an unfavorable outcome in response to good behavior. For instance, if Kasey doesn't say anything inappropriate to us for a week we will unblock him on Facebook.

We do not have to learn these terms: we just have to remember that we have a number of options to choose from, some punitive and some not so much, some subtle and some overt. We can pick the punishments and reinforcers most likely to maximize our chances of getting what we want at the lowest possible cost. If our first choice doesn't work out, we can try something else.

Positive punishments don't need to be extreme (or, as in the case of punching Kasey in the nuts, potentially illegal) in order to work. In a creep-averse environment, merely saying out loud "get your hand off my leg *now*" could be enough of a positive punishment to teach Kasey that that behavior is a bad idea: his resulting loss of status will have a negative impact on him. In a creep-friendly environment, however, that approach will likely do us very little good.

Physical positive punishments, particularly violent ones, carry the risk of escalation. If Kasey "only" touched us, and in response we slapped him, we have escalated the encounter; whether he decides that it's OK for him to slap us back will depend on a number of factors, some of which we may not be aware of. We will also be fighting against the "Slap-Slap-Kiss" trope,[15] which dictates that a physical escalation between potential sexual partners will invariably result in sex. As tropes go, this one won't win any prizes for being logical or well-rooted in reality, but enough people believe in it that we can't discount it. There are guys who will see any physical engagement on our part as a step bedward, even if our action is anything but a come-on.

Punishment by removal is a much safer choice, both in terms of our physical safety and in the way it conveys our intentions. Kasey can't bother us, let alone hurt us, if we're nowhere near him. It's also harder for someone to interpret the fact that every time he walks into a room we walk out as a come-on; it's not impossible, but it takes a special kind of person. Any third parties watching will also be unlikely to construe it as an odd flirtation.

The removal doesn't have to be physical. We can block Kasey's number or unfriend him online. We don't have to remove ourselves, either: maybe Kasey will be disinvited from any future activity we organize.

This is critical: we will probably have to explain the connection between the behavior and the punishment to Kasey and to everyone else watching, particularly if the two don't take place immediately after each other. There is an obvious immediacy to us slapping someone who pinches our bum. That immediacy is missing if our punishment is not inviting Kasey to our party next Friday because of what he said last Tuesday. Unless we are explaining what we are doing and why, nobody, Kasey included, will be

---

[15] http://tvtropes.org/pmwiki/pmwiki.php/Main/SlapSlapKiss

any the wiser.

Depending on how we frame it and who gets to know about it, explaining that we are punishing Kasey could be an added punishment: it potentially engages our entire social group in the process. Whether that has a positive overall effect will depend on how our social group operates. If we find ourselves in a creep haven, privately letting each individual member know about the issue may work better than bringing it out into the open. Even though no other member may be willing to openly support us, the fact that they are aware of our problem may be to our advantage. Communication shines a light on the creep's actions.

Operant conditioning is a very mechanistic way of interacting with people, but it has the distinctive advantage of being generally effective. We can combine punishments and reinforcements that suit our situation in order to obtain the behavior we consider acceptable. Provided that we are consistent, we may be able to retrain Kasey in behaving in a way we deem acceptable, or force him to realize that he is not going to get what he wants from being around us and go creeping elsewhere. This is particularly likely to happen if the rest of our group supports us and our efforts. If the group as a whole is inconsistent with punishing and reinforcing behaviors, Kasey's behavior may only improve around us, or not at all.

Operant conditioning can also be used against us, particularly if we aren't aware of how it works. Creeps can train us and our group to tolerate worsening behaviors by punishing any criticism and reinforcing acquiescence. The social forces that operate around us can do the same, as we have already covered. Turning a blind eye to the misbehavior of difficult people while punishing good people when they try to take a stand against it is the path of least resistance: difficult people are harder to punish than good people. It's easier to keep a well-behaved child on the naughty step.

60% OF THE TIME, IT WORKS EVERY TIME

Although they may seem daunting if we are not used to them, boundary setting and operant conditioning are extremely versatile skills that get easier with practice. We can practice them in safe settings until they become almost a habit, and that practice will help us use them in more difficult situations.

At some point, however, we may come to a situation where these techniques aren't a viable option. Many difficult people are difficult because they know they can act out safely. People who can be punished for their misbehavior in some way, any way, usually learn to self-regulate. People only need to be told off, fined, sacked, thrown out, shunned, or punched in the nuts so many times before they learn their lesson. Some people, however, are so privileged they are almost untouchable. A lot of that privilege comes with status or with money: unfair as it may seem, some people are powerful enough to escape even legal repercussions, let alone social ones.

There are also people so uninterested in the benefits social relations bring that they are hard to punish. They don't care about being told off or shunned. They couldn't care about being ostracized by society at large, let alone by us. No punishment we could inflict registers with them.

The correlation between difficult people and people who can't be easily punished is not a coincidence: many people are only difficult when they can get away with it. They may have been the easiest-going, pleasantest people we knew until they managed to get in a position from which they have some power over us, and then they showed their other side. This applies in a variety of settings, from a pleasant colleague turning into a creepy boss the moment he got his promotion, to a romantic partner getting us to get married, quit our job, move away from our family, have a child, before demonstrating how much of a misogynist he is.

Sometimes we only know the truth about people when it's hard to do something about it. That isn't because we were oblivious up to that point. Some people genuinely have two (or more) faces, and only show us the one they want us to see.

We should also bear in mind that, unless we are problem people, most of our problems will occur when we are dealing with problem people. We will not find ourselves struggling to defend our boundaries from respectful people who have healthy boundaries. We won't have to protect ourselves from consent violations by people who are invested in consent. If we were dealing with someone on the same page as us, these kinds of issues would not arise – or, if they did, they would be resolved so quickly and willingly that they wouldn't be issues at all. The fact that we need to fight our corner proves that we are in difficult waters, dealing with someone who doesn't play by our rules.

Some of the perpetrators of these transgressions are people who know the rules and deliberately choose to break them for their convenience – negligent or malignant creeps, perhaps even criminals. Some, however, will be people who cannot parse the rules or somehow believe that they're optional extras. The latter can be infinitely harder to deal with, even though they don't even mean to do anything bad. Criminals, unless they're newbies, tend to act like professionals. They assess whether picking on us is worth it based on the perceived risk/reward ratio. If we can tip the ratio in our favor, they may respond by giving up. Chances are that they'll give up on us and try and victimize someone else, because that's what they do, but for our intents and purposes the problem will be over.

Not so with people who fail to parse the basic dynamics of social interactions. We express a request, and they ignore it. We issue a demand, and they ignore it. We threaten a repercussion, and they ignore it. We exact the repercussion, and they move on to doing something else at us. They don't get the point. It's like punching treacle. In the same way that pain compliance doesn't work against someone who doesn't feel pain, social repercussions do not work against someone who operates in their own little world. Carrying out antisocial repercussions against them can land us in serious trouble. This is particularly true if it makes us the ones escalating the situation; for instance, if the problem wasn't physical, and we made it so. We can end up in an endless struggle against someone who doesn't even understand that we are struggling.

A lot of handy tips on how to deal with difficult people assume that the people in question have normal responses to stimuli. That's often not the case. The person who pesters us with dozens of messages may stop when we tell them to... or they may carry on. They may stop when we stop replying... or they may carry on. They may disappear when we block them or change our number... or they may find us on social media. They may give up when we block and report them... or they may proceed to create false account after false account just so they can continue to contact us.[16] If we disappear from all virtual communications, they may give up... or they may decide that they need to find where we live to make sure that we are OK. And none of this is because we didn't handle the situation right: it's because that tool doesn't work against that person, because their responses aren't normal. This should be obvious from the start, because normal people do not deluge people with messages.

There is also a rare minority of people who are incorrigible because they don't "get" punishment. They are unable to draw any line between their actions and any imposed consequences. They never got spanked because they stole a cookie: they always got spanked because mom was big enough to spank them and wanted to. They never got sent to prison for assault; they always got sent to prison because that's what judges like to do. They are incapable of seeing their own actions as part of the chain of events.

The chances of us encountering this type of person are low, but it can happen. This shouldn't discourage us from trying to manage them or cause us to give up. It should remind us to be gentle with ourselves when we review our performance. Sometimes things are difficult – not just difficult for us, because we're crap at them, but objectively difficult. And if this kind of problem was simple to manage, it wouldn't be so damn common.

---

[16] Before you go on about "yeahbut if someone behaves like that you just call the police on them", consider what chances you may have of getting help from the authorities when your complaint is "this person, to whom I willingly gave my contact details, continues to ask me if I would like some pizza." And before you go on about "but how could that be a problem", consider how you'd feel if you'd told that person to cut it out and leave you alone three dozen times, and still they carried on.

REVIEW AND DEBRIEF

Once we have done whatever we were going to do, we need to review our results. There are three main options:
- Our problem went away.
- Our problem didn't go away.
- Our problem changed.

If the problem went away, we may never find out why. Did we teach a socially awkward person how to function better? Did we put a creep off? All we know is that the behavior no longer affects us. If this resolution comes without much effort on our part, we may wonder whether we ever had a problem at all.

The problem with self-defense is that it is a negative feedback system: if it works well, nothing happens. That kind of result can be very difficult to analyze. Did Kasey stop bugging us because we were so good at setting boundaries, or did he never mean to bug us in the first place? There's no way to know. We could spend a lifetime analyzing each moment and never come to a definite conclusion.

We do know, however, that we no longer have a problem. That is something to be celebrated. We may still want to keep a close eye on Kasey, in case the problem has just moved along and he's pestering someone else (a clear red flag), or to stop him coming at us again from a different angle. We may never be 100% confident that he is 100% safe to be around. What we did, though, is an achievement. If it was difficult for us, that's a huge achievement: we have stepped out of our comfort zone to deal with an issue, and we prevailed. If it was easy for us, that's also a huge achievement: it indicates that we can navigate the waters of awkward social situations.

If the problem did not go away, that doesn't mean that we failed. We selected a strategy based on the available information, and that strategy was not successful: that adds to the information available to us. **Every decision is an experiment:** we have never made it before, and we don't know beforehand what results it will bring.

We will need to pick our next step. Do we want to escalate, and how? Is bailing out our best option? Either way, chances are that there will be costs. The further we have to escalate, the greater the potential costs.

This is the time to start creating a paper trail, literally or figuratively. Whether in a diary, spreadsheet, computer calendar, or any other media, we can jot down a brief summary of our interactions with Kasey: where and when we met him, what happened, and any witnesses. If any of our communications are in writing, we can keep copies in a dedicated folder. If his behavior ever escalates to an actionable level, our list of his prior misbehaviors will support our case. If we ever have to escalate with him to the point of doing something that could get us in trouble, having a record of past problems will support our case.

If our goal is for Kasey to leave us alone altogether, we need to tell him, clearly and firmly, that his attention is unwanted and that he is to stop all contact. For the purpose of creating a paper trail, this should be done in writing (email or text will do), and we will need to keep a copy of that communication. After we have done so, we will need to follow four golden rules:

- Have no contact him, even to reiterate that we don't want to talk to him. We should not give him any attention at all. If we ignore 50 of his messages and blow our top at the 51st, all we've done is teach him that it takes 50 messages to get our attention.
- Tell others. If the people around us aren't aware that we are having this problem, they will not keep an eye out for us and they might inadvertently give him information that will give him more access to us, such as a new phone number or the name of the new gym we attend.
- Review our safety arrangements at home, at work, and anywhere else we may go to. Many creeps are cowards who do not practice or plan for physical escalations, but that doesn't mean that they can't be physically dangerous. If they have the opportunity to physically attack their prey without fear of retribution, they may opt to do so. If they are pushed into a physical confrontation, they may fight back, and they may turn out to be powerful opponents. If they are punished for their actions, they may seek revenge. We do not have to obsess about this kind of event, but if we are aware that there are gaps in our safety arrangements, this is a good time to fill them up.
- Collect evidence. The evidence needs to be as comprehensive and as organized as possible, in the event that things escalate to a point where we can get the authorities involved. We might want to create a designated space to store the evidence – a journal, a dedicated folder for print-outs, or a folder in our phone for emails and messages. Not only will this grant us easy access to what we need in case we need it, but it will also mean that the evidence is not right under our noses at all times, needlessly upsetting us.

This is the worst-case scenario. Chances are that our situation will never degenerate to this point. However, if it does, we will know what to do. That in itself may give us the businesslike, confident manner that keeps many a creep at bay.

Sometime a creep may change his behavior so that it respects our stated boundaries, but it still makes us feel comfortable. In that case we will have to repeat the entire process to address the new issue.

In some cases the creep might act as if our exchange created some kind of special bond between us. This may be an honest feeling on his part, but it doesn't create an obligation on ours: just because we "cured" him, it doesn't mean that we have to adopt him or befriend him. If this behavior is problematic, we may need to repeat the boundary setting process.

Some guys operate under the assumption that respecting women entitles them to some kind of boon, usually a sexual one. They treat sex as if it was the prize for completing a reward chart: "I wasn't awful to you ten times in a row! That entitles me to at least a blow-job!" The mindset would be funnier if it weren't so prevalent. Needless to say, this attitude is neither acceptable nor safe. We should not tolerate it.

The most important part of the review process is that it's not supposed to be a rod we beat ourselves with. Sometimes we "win," sometimes we learn. When we get really lucky we do both. If we found the process hard, we definitely learnt something. If we found the process easy, we worked on our confidence. If we totally fudged it, we learnt what we need to work on. Whatever happened, the fact that we're still here to review it means that we didn't mess up that badly. It is infinitely more helpful for us to think "I've made a mistake, I'm still learning" than "I've made a mistake, I'm a total idiot and everyone must despise me." We've already got to deal with assholes; we don't need to give one shelter in our cranium.

AFTERCARE

Regardless of how the process went, we are likely to experience some feelings about it. We may feel shaken up, depressed, elated, or anything in between. In the immediate aftermath, we may be adrenalized.

Adrenaline is a hormone and neurotransmitter naturally present in our bodies. In response to stress, several chemical compounds, including adrenaline, are released directly into the bloodstream – what we call for simplicity's sake the *adrenaline dump*. This sudden chemical change affects both our bodies and our minds.

The possible effects of adrenaline are covered in details in Rory Miller's "Meditations on Violence: A Comparison of Martial Arts Training & Real World Violence." In brief, adrenaline can do any combination of the following:

- Increase our heart rate and blood pressure.
- Increase our speed and strength.
- Decrease sensitivity to pain.
- Decrease coordination.
- Decrease blood flow to the surface of the skin.
- Cause tunnel vision.
- Reduce hearing.
- Cloud thinking.
- Affect perception of time (everything slows down).
- Cause repetitive behavior loops (e.g. repeating the same sentence or hitting in the same way, even though it is not working).

These chemical effects do not end when the emergency does. Women in particular commonly experience a delayed reaction minutes or even hours after the event: we might get the shakes, cry uncontrollably, feel nauseated, or throw up. We may also feel suddenly and inexplicably sexually aroused. All of this may look like an emotional reaction, but it's actually the result of sudden chemical changes. Men can react in similar ways, but they go through the effects much faster, so this phase is often less noticeable with them because it takes place while they are still busy dealing with the event or its immediate aftermath.

We need to be aware that we may experience these delayed physiological reactions, and that they are purely the result of hormones coursing through our blood stream. If we start "crying over nothing" an hour or two after the event, we are not having hysterics or a nervous breakdown: we're merely riding a hormonal rollercoaster.

Even if we do not experience an adrenal dump, we may feel a bit up-

and-down about it all. This is a good time for us to take care of ourselves, to do whatever we do to relax – take a hot bath, go for a run, eat takeaway in lieu of cooking, punch a bag, pet a puppy, visit grandma, whatever works for us.

It is also a good time to get someone to take care of us. If we have partners, family members, or friends who are good in this kind of situation, we might want to enlist their help. We might not be in the mood for a celebration – though we deserve one, because we did something difficult – but the opportunity to talk it all out with caring, positive people can do us a world of good.

It can do them good, too. What we have just done is something that many women struggle with – if this weren't the case, creeps would be extinct. By sharing our experience with other women, we can help them gain the confidence to stand up against creeps. By sharing it with men, we can help them be more aware of a side of humanity they would otherwise be blissfully oblivious of.

What we did was a good thing – not just for us, but for women in general. The more we talk about this, the more opportunities we give ourselves to spread awareness, share information, broaden our skill set, or just commiserate. Chances are that most of the women we know will have gone through this kind of experience, and those who haven't would benefit from hearing about it. We are not alone in this unless we make ourselves so by our silence.

RECAP

We may not know what kind of creep we are dealing with, or even if we are dealing with a creep at all. However, it doesn't matter, because the same solutions work regardless.

The only thing we need to do to derail the creep script is not to follow it. Whatever our response is, provided that it isn't the expected freezing and compliance, it will thwart the creep's plans.

If we want to take a more constructive solution, we will need to use our words to state our problem and request a change in behavior.

Boundary setting is a four-phase process:

- **Set**. We decide what the boundary is going to be.
- **Ask**. We clearly request a change in behavior.
- **Tell**. We repeat the request and present the consequences of not respecting it.
- **Consequences**. We do exactly as we said we'd do.

Without consequences, boundary setting is just begging.

We can use **Operant Conditioning** to modify a creep's behavior. By reinforcing good behavior and not reinforcing bad behavior, we can push the behavior in the right direction until it meets our requirements.

If our efforts are successful, we will no longer have a problem. If they are not, that is not a sign of failure: we conducted an experiment and obtained a result. Now we have more information about our problem, information we can use to reassess it and create a better strategy to deal with it.

Regardless of how the process goes, chances are that we will have some feelings about it. We may be adrenalized. This is a good time to take extra care of ourselves, or to let someone take care of us.

Discussing the events with someone we trust may help us process them faster. It will also give people a chance to learn from our experience. The only way to spread awareness of this issue is to talk about it.

This may all sound more easily said than done, and it is. However, it is doable, and the more we do it, the easier it gets. These difficulties and the fact that it takes effort to overcome them don't just affect us. This issue is ubiquitous *because* it is so very rarely dealt with. If we all stood up against creeps, their game would stop working. By looking out for this kind of behavior and addressing it when it comes up, we are not only going to improve our own lives, but potentially also those of the people around us.

CREEPOLOGY AND NEURODIVERGENCE

When it comes to dealing with creeps, sexual predators, and intimate-partner abusers, the impact of neurodivergence can be so significant that it deserves its own chapter. This is not because neurodivergence makes us inherently weaker or less able to fend for ourselves. Some neurodivergent traits do play a part in this issue, but the bulk of the problem is caused by the impact of being neurodivergent in a predominantly neurotypical society. The issue is two-fold: one the one hand, neurodivergents may be perceived as lower-risk targets for would-be abusers, which increases our chances of being picked on. On the other hand, we might find it harder to deal with these situations once they arise because of our early training and an ongoing scarcity of social resources.

Not all neurodivergent people experience the same symptoms or live the same lives, so it's impossible to generalize the neurodivergent experience, but these are some of the factors in play:

1. REJECTION SENSITIVE DYSPHORIA.

Rejection-Sensitive dysphoria is "the disposition to anxiously expect, readily perceive, and intensely react to rejection." Up to 99% of teens and adults with ADHD are more sensitive than their neurotypical peers to rejection, and nearly 1 in 3 say it's the hardest part of living with ADHD.[17] RSD can have a profound impact on a person's ability and willingness to engage in social interactions. People may "adapt" by becoming hostile, socially withdrawn, or over-accommodating of others.[18]

RSD is not a currently recognized condition.[19] It might also not be a condition in its own right, or a symptom of neurodivergence, but a reaction to maltreatment or attachment failures in childhood.[20] In essence, RSD may be a response to the trauma of being neurodivergent in a neurotypical world and the attendant social difficulties, rather than a

---

[17] https://www.webmd.com/add-adhd/rejection-sensitive-dysphoria
[18] https://www.ncbi.nlm.nih.gov/pmc/articles/PMC2771869/
[19] https://www.healthline.com/health/mental-health/rejection-sensitive-dysphoria
[20] https://psycnet.apa.org/record/1997-36663-003

result of our neurodivergence in and of itself.

RSD can impact our ability to respond to toxic behaviors for two main reasons. Firstly, we can be incredibly frightened of any kind of upheaval in our social group. Given how often whistleblowers are punished or ostracized, being wary of putting ourselves in that position when we know how crushing the resulting RSD will be is a reasonable concern. Secondly, we have a tendency to assume that other people will be equally crushed by criticism and rejection. We may resist giving out negative responses in order to spare people's feelings, or soft-pedal our statements to the point of uselessness, particularly when we are dealing with people who have no interest in respecting our boundaries.

2. WE ARE TRAINED TO SUPPRESS AND DISCOUNT OUR FEELINGS.

Some neurodivergent people struggle with emotional self-regulation. We may suffer from low frustration tolerance, temper outbursts, emotional impulsivity, and mood lability (rapid, often exaggerated changes in mood). In a nutshell, we have a lot of feelings and struggle to hide them.

While learning to manage our emotions is an essential part of being a functional human being, there is a difference between learning to feel a feeling without acting upon it, and learning to suppress or to discount the feeling. Suppressing feelings may make our lives smoother and simpler, but it cuts us off from a very important source of information. In the context of abusive relationships, suppressing our feelings can make us slow to react to toxic situations, both in the short- and long-term. We may not respond to the fear we feel when a predator targets us, or the icky feeling of dealing with a creep. We may also remain in an unhealthy relationship because we have lost access to the signals that would inform us that the relationship is unhealthy.

Doubting our feelings also makes us susceptible to gaslighting – "a form of persistent manipulation and brainwashing that causes the victim to doubt her or himself, and ultimately lose her or his own sense of perception, identity, and self-worth."[21] In a very real sense, by ignoring or suppressing our feelings, we are gaslighting ourselves: we are teaching ourselves that our perception of reality is incorrect and should be ignored.

---

[21] https://www.psychologytoday.com/gb/blog/communication-success/201704/7-stages-gaslighting-in-relationship

When someone who purports to love us does the same, we can fall for it without a moment's hesitation.

3. WE ARE SCARED OF ALL THINGS AWKWARD.

Many neurodivergent people are accustomed to social gaffes. We are emotional, we are impulsive, we are often loud, and words have a tendency to fall out of our mouths (or keyboards) before we have had a chance to apply any kind of filter. We know all about Foot-in-Mouth disease, and we know how much it hurts. This can make us way too tolerant of people who mess up "just like us."

Unfortunately, some people mess up on purpose. For instance, creeps and predators enjoy making us feel uncomfortable or frightened. Abusers enjoy making us feel inferior and powerless. Other people may not mess up on purpose, but mess up in ways that can be very harmful (i.e., people who don't fully understand consent, or who have been brought up to think that "no means maybe", etc.). These people do not respond to subtle hints; if we want their behavior to change, we need to set clear boundaries and enforce them as needed; if that fails, we need to leave the situation.

But what if it turns out that the person we thought was a creep is just awkward? What if they never meant to upset us at all, and our reaction triggers their RSD? What if we set those boundaries, and the person gets upset at us, and everyone finds out, and the whole situation degenerates until our entire social group falls apart around us? Just thinking about that can trigger our RSD.

Our reluctance to put our foot in it until we're absolutely sure that we are dealing with a problem person can put us in grave danger. If we are facing a physical predator, we might find ourselves having to fight our way out of a situation we could have avoided. If we are dealing with a non-physical predator such as a creep, we might end up suffering in silence for long periods of time, never quite feeling safe but never giving ourselves permission to ensure our safety. If we are dealing with an abuser, we might give them the opportunity to cause profound damage to our bodies, minds, and social networks, which will make it harder for us to stop the abuse.

4. WE ARE DOPAMINE FIENDS.

Some neurodivergences (most notably ADHD) have been linked to low dopamine levels.[22] Dopamine is a feel-good hormone: it is responsible for

---

[22] https://www.healthline.com/health/adhd/adhd-dopamine#connection

feelings of pleasure and reward, and allows us to regulate emotional responses and take action to achieve specific goals.

Dopamine levels shoot up in the early parts of a relationship,[23] and peter off over time as the relationship stabilizes. Alas, dopamine levels also increase in response to stress.[24] As a result, we may meet someone and get a shot of dopamine not because they are The One, but because they are A Wrong'Un, and we might be unable to tell the difference.

5. WHIRLWIND ROMANCE OR LOVE BOMBING?

Love bombing is the practice of "overwhelming someone with signs of adoration and attraction (...) designed to manipulate you into spending more time with the bomber."[25] Basically, it's setting off on a relationship way too fast and too intensely with the specific purpose of getting someone hooked on you before they really know you well enough to realize that actually you're a manipulative douche.

Thing is, for a lot of neurodivergent people falling head over heels is the normal way to start a relationship. We are fast, we are impulsive, we can hyperfocus on people just as much as we do on anything else, and we love that sweet, sweet dopamine that a new relationship gives us. For us, though, that's not a tactic: it's just the way our brain and heart work.

When we cross romantic paths with a manipulative love-bomber, we may fail to realize that there is a problem because the two behaviors are, on the outside, quite similar. It's only the motivations that vary. By the time those motivations are uncovered, we may find ourselves in a very bad situation.

6. WE ARE ACCUSTOMED TO BEING PUNISHED IN THE NAME OF LOVE.

On average, children with ADHD receive a full 20,000 more "negative messages" in their lifetimes than their neurotypical cohort.[26] On the one hand, that makes sense: we struggle to behave properly. On the other hand... we just *can't* behave properly. We don't choose to be distracted, easily bored, forgetful, impulsive, fidgety, hyperfocused on the wrong

---

[23] https://neuro.hms.harvard.edu/harvard-mahoney-neuroscience-institute/brain-newsletter/and-brain/love-and-brain

[24] https://www.jneurosci.org/content/24/11/2825

[25] https://www.psychologytoday.com/us/blog/lifetime-connections/201804/love-bombing-narcissists-secret-weapon

[26] https://www.additudemag.com/children-with-adhd-avoid-failure-punishment/

things, perennially late, and so on and so forth. These are not things we choose to do: they are symptoms of our neurodivergence, and all we can do is learn how to work around them. Scolding a child with ADHD for spacing out is not unlike scolding a short-sighted child for failing to read something on the board: you are punishing them for something they have no control over, and for the way they are. This is particularly fun for those kids with RSD, for whom the knowledge of having done wrong is in itself a punishment.

When this punishment is routinely presented as being "for our own good", we may end up buying into that. We may learn to believe that being cared for means getting hurt, and that the people who love us should punish us for our transgressions, regardless of their causes. If that doesn't prime us for abuse later on in life, nothing else will.

This issue is compounded for neurodivergent people who are put through systematic abuse in childhood in order to "cure" them of their neurodivergence. For instance, many of the common "therapies" aimed at autistic children inhibit their ability to respond to negative stimuli, to display their needs and wants, or to interact with their environment and with other people in ways they find natural, comfortable, and rewarding. In order to achieve these dubious goals, some of these therapies foster a relationship between patient and provider that is inherently abusive: the provider has the power to withhold what the patient needs to feel safe and comfortable, and only allows the patient to access it as a reward for behaving in a certain manner. As often as not, the required behavior is unnatural, uncomfortable, or even painful for the patient. In a nutshell, in order to stop hurting, the child has to do something that hurts – and all of this is done in an allegedly caring context, with parental support, and for the child's own good. Needless to say, this type of early training can severely harm those forced through it, and can impact their ability to protect themselves from other forms of abuse later on in life.

7. WE BELIEVE THAT THERE IS SOMETHING INHERENTLY WRONG WITH US.

This is connected to the above point, but it's its own thing. Being constantly told that there is something wrong with us can, unsurprisingly, lead us to believe that there is something wrong with us. This is particularly true for those of us who are diagnosed later on in life, because we don't even have the comfort of a diagnosis to explain to us what's going on, and to help us work around it.

Being constantly exposed to a barrage of negative comments can turn us into people-pleasers. We try to make up for our perceived shortcomings by doing whatever it takes to make people like us, even when it has a negative impact on our life. When other people's behavior hurts us, we may ignore that hurt and accept it as the price of admission in the relationship. When our world is hurting us, we try to change ourselves instead of trying to change the world. If part of that hurt is caused by being in a relationship with an abuser, that can take us to very bad places.

8. WE HAVE UNSUPPORTIVE SUPPORT NETWORKS.

Many neurotypical people are more emotional than the average person. That doesn't mean that we feel the wrong emotions! We may just feel them more intensely, or struggle to modulate our reaction to them. Unfortunately, our emotionality can lead to the people in our lives discounting not only our feelings about our problems, but the problems themselves. We are probably making a mountain out of a molehill. It can't really be that bad. It probably wasn't that bad to start with, and we made it worse by overreacting. Hell, it's probably our fault: if we could just calm down and act like normal people...

The result is that if we find ourselves in a difficult or even dangerous situation, we might find ourselves unable to get any help from our social network. By the time we have accumulated enough evidence to support our concerns, we may have gotten needlessly hurt.

This list is neither comprehensive nor universal. Not all of these factors apply to all neurodivergent people. Furthermore, some neurodivergent people are affected by additional factors that impact their ability to deal with creeps, predators, and abusers. Basically, anything that increases our ability to identify and respond to inappropriate behavior will affect our ability to deal with creeps, while anything that lowers our social capital will make it riskier for us to take the necessary steps to resolve the issue. This doesn't mean that neurodivergent people are doomed to be victims; we can learn to do what we need to do, and work towards building a social group that supports us when we have to do it. It can be hard work, though, and it pays to acknowledge that. Dealing with creeps is hard for most people, but it can be extra hard for us, and that's not our fault. The playing field just isn't level. Even if nobody else does, we can respect that, and we can be proud of our efforts and our struggles.

Your Toolkit

"*Imitate an instructor and the best you can ever hope for is to become a flawed clone of someone else. But work on you, and you can become better than your teacher. Not the same, better.*"
– Rory Miller

WORKBOOK

Your experience with creeps is unique to you, as are the resources you have to deal with the problem.

In order to maximize your chances of getting what you want from your anti-creep strategies, you need to determine:

- Where you draw the line on creeps. What are you willing to tolerate? What behaviors or motivations will you excuse?
- What your goals and priorities are. What does a "win" look like?
- What your best strategy is for achieving your goals, based on your resources and preferences.

What is YOUR definition of a creep?

....

....

....

....

....

Do you know anyone meeting that description?

1. ....

2. ....

3. ....

4. ....

What are the two most common reasons for creeping?

1. ....

2. ....

Are you willing to tolerate them?

1. ....

2. ....

What characteristics make a space a creep haven?

1. ....
2. ....
3. ....
4. ....

List any spaces you frequent which display those characteristics:

1. ....
2. ....
3. ....
4. ....
5. ....
6. ....
7. ....
8. ....

What are five red flags for creeping?

1. ....
2. ....
3. ....
4. ....
5. ....

List a real-life example for each red flag:

1. ....
2. ....
3. ....
4. ....
5. ....

Your natural responses to conflict are:

1. ....
2. ....
3. ....

In the stereotypical creep script:

They: ....
You: ....
They: ....

In your ideal creep script:

They: ....
You: ....
They: ....

Ways to derail the creep script:

1. ....
2. ....
3. ....
4. ....
5. ....
6. ....
7. ....
8. ....
9. ....
10. ....
11. ....
12. ....

GLOSSARY

This is a list of terms I use in this book. It is a glossary of *concepts*, not of legal or official terms. Some of these terms are neologisms with no legal definitions, while others have legal definitions that vary between locations.

Creep: a person who **consciously** behaves in a manner likely to give someone an unpleasant feeling of fear or unease, specifically where there is a sexual undercurrent to that discomfort.

Negligent Creep: a person who behaves in ways that he knows may creep women out on the off-chance that it might get him laid.

Negligent creeps put their own sexual desires ahead of other people's interests and comfort. Their goal is seduction, not revulsion, but the revulsion they cause doesn't stop them. They just don't care enough.

Malignant Creep: a low-level sexual predator who creeps people out consciously and deliberately.

Malignant creeps engage in certain behaviors because they know that it will make women feel repulsed or threatened. They are bona fide predators, even if they never go physical. They are doing as much as they can to get their kicks without doing anything they could be punished for.

Socially Awkward: someone whose public behavior falls outside of the social norm.

Social awkwardness can be the symptom of a number of underlying causes (e.g. unconventional socialization, social anxiety, autism, personality disorders, mental health issues, etc.). Some socially awkward people respond positively to explicit verbal cues, while some don't.

Asshole: "the guy who systematically allows himself special advantages in cooperative life out of an entrenched sense of entitlement that immunizes him against the complaints of other people."[27]

Social capital: the people we know and the benefits we reap from our mutual support (reciprocity). This support could take many forms: physical, financial, emotional, psychological, social, etc.

---

[27] https://www.philosophersmag.com/essays/76-the-meaning-of-asshole

Sexual harassment: any unwanted behavior of a sexual nature that we find offensive or which makes us feel distressed, intimidated or humiliated.

Sexual assault: any type of sexual contact or behavior that occurs without the explicit consent of the recipient.

Rape: penetration, no matter how slight, of the vagina or anus with any body part or object, or oral penetration by a sex organ of another person, without the consent of the victim.

Consent: "compliance in or approval of what is done or proposed by another; specifically the voluntary agreement or acquiescence by a person of age or with requisite mental capacity who is not under duress or coercion and usually who has knowledge or understanding compliance in or approval of what is done or proposed by another."[28]

There is no consensus as yet on what criteria sexual consent should encompass. My favorite standards are those put forward by Planned Parenthood[29]:

"Understanding consent is as easy as F.R.I.E.S.

Consent is:

Freely given: Doing something sexual with someone is a decision that should be made without pressure, force, manipulation, or while drunk or high.

Reversible: Anyone can change their mind about what they want to do, at any time. Even if you've done it before or are in the middle of having sex.

Informed: Be honest. For example, if someone says they'll use a condom and then they don't, that's not consent.

Enthusiastic: If someone isn't excited, or really into it, that's not consent.

Specific: Saying yes to one thing (like going to the bedroom to make out) doesn't mean they've said yes to others (like oral sex)."

Gaslighting: manipulation that seeks to sow seeds of doubt, hoping to make the targets question their own memory, perception, and sanity.[30]

---

[28] https://www.merriam-webster.com/dictionary/consent

[29] http://plannedparenthood.tumblr.com/post/148506806862/understanding-consent-is-as-easy-as-fries-consent

[30] https://en.wikipedia.org/wiki/Gaslighting

FURTHER READING

"**Conflict Communications – A functional taxonomy of human conflict**" by Rory Miller. It's a powerful tool that can help you communicate more effectively while avoiding and navigating conflict.

"**Meditations on Violence: A Comparison of Martial Arts Training & Real World Violence**" by Rory Miller. This book is probably the best introduction to the complexity of the reality of violence and its potential effects on survivors.

"**Violence: A Writer's Guide**" by Rory Miller. Although designed to explain violence to writers, it is a good introduction to anyone who has limited or no first-hand experience on the subject.

"**Emotional Abuse: A manual for self-defense**" by Zak Mucha. Explains in a succinct yet comprehensive manner the mechanisms and impacts of emotional abuse and how a history of abuse can facilitate future abuse.

"**Nonviolent Communication – A Language of Life**" by Marshall B. Rosenberg. A non-confrontational approach to communicating needs and resolving conflicts. It routinely fails to work on cock-roaches and a number of other problem people. However, precisely because of that, it can be used to help identify them.

"**Complex PTSD: From Surviving to Thriving**" by Pete Walker. It explains in detail the different responses to stress and conflict (freeze, flight, fight, fawn) and their drawbacks.

"**The Gift of Fear: Survival Signals That Protect Us from Violence**" by Gavin de Becker. It aims to teach us to use our natural intuition to spot and react to danger signs. I found it informative, but somewhat sensationalistic and potentially triggering.

https://www.stalkingriskprofile.com/ A website designed for professionals working with victims or perpetrators of stalking, full of well-presented, concise advice.

ABOUT THE AUTHOR

There are self-defense instructors who are the living embodiment of humanity's ability to triumph over monumental adversities. I am not one of them. There are instructors who have dedicated years of their lives to the study of martial arts or self-defense techniques. I'm not one of them either. There are those who, after witnessing the real-life impact of abnormal psychology on people's lives, went on to study the issue professionally. I didn't do that. There are those who willingly put themselves in danger to protect others, day after day, even though the fully understand the potential costs. I know I'd suck at that, so I don't even try. There are those who are seeking to create a community of people they can guide towards a brighter future. That is definitely a nope from me.

There is nothing epic, mythical, or mystical about me. I'm the bastard child of a lowest-middle-class family. I grew up in a somewhat rough-ish environment (a picnic compared to a lot of kids' lives), went feral-ish in my teens (but skirted around any real trouble), and have travelled a bit (but I'm still missing 3 continents, unless you count stopovers). I'm under 5' tall and practically made of tits, so I'm ostensibly most predators' ideal victim. That has at times added a modicum of excitement to my life, but no biggie. Occasionally I do stuff like running off with the circus and people get very excited about it, but I don't get the hype: unless that's something you want to do, my experience will not help you.

The only thing remotely remarkable about me is that I have thus far managed to survive my own decision-making process. I'm dented, but I'm still here as I write this. (I'm also superstitious enough to worry about whether I'll still be here as you read it, in case I jinxed myself: how's that for a maturity fail?) The bottom line is that if you're looking for wisdom, inspiration, or guidance, then you need to look elsewhere. It ain't me you're looking for. And no, I'm not using reverse psychology.

The only reason I ever got to publishing non-fiction is that there are three things I know better than most "normal" people. I've just happened to be (un)lucky enough to be able to collect a combination of knowledge and experience that apparently gives me an edge on literally three subjects. If that sounds like a very limited purview, it's because it is.

Putting what I knew in writing and sticking out there so people may not have to learn from their own trials and errors seemed like a good idea at the time. It doesn't make me an authority figure, in general or on the subjects at hand. This book sums up one of the three things I know. Given the subject matter, I hope it's perfectly useless to you: I hope that everything I'm talking about remains so distant from your life as to be purely conceptual. But hey, if you ever need this stuff, it's in here.

If you found this useful, please check out:

https://godsbastard.wordpress.com/

Made in the USA
Middletown, DE
08 May 2022

65489934R00068